The Forgotten Generation

The Forgotten Generation

American Children and World War II

Lisa L. Ossian

University of Missouri Press
Columbia

University of Missouri Press
Columbia and London

University of Missouri Press, Columbia, Missouri 65211
Printed and bound in the United States of America

First paperback printing, 2021

Cataloging-in-Publication data available from the Library of Congress.

ISBN : 978-0-8262-2234-3 (paperback : alk. paper)
ISBN : 978-0-8262-1919-0 (hardcover : alk. paper)

∞™ This paper meets the requirements of the
American National Standard for Permanence of Paper
for Printed Library Materials, Z39.48, 1984.

Design and composition: K. Lee Design & Graphics
Typefaces: Palatino and Trebuchet

Chapter 4, "Junior Commandos," is adapted from a chapter in Lisa M. DeTora, ed., *Heroes of Film, Comics, and American Culture: Essays on Real and Fictional Defenders of Home,* © 2009 by permission of McFarland & Company, Inc., Jefferson, NC 28640.

To Roger and Susan Ossian,
my parents, fans, and critics

Contents

Preface

The Paradox of Children

It was a paradoxical alignment of principles and priorities, and the more Americans emphasized the importance of their own rights and goals, the less they regarded or respected the rights or even the lives of groups of people they considered to be "others."

—Kerry A. Trask, *Black Hawk: The Battle for the Heart of America* (2006)

A child's world always has had odd dimensions, as narrow as the backyard or a corner of the kitchen, but as broad as the imagination.

—Reed Karaim, "A New Era in Play," *USA Weekend* (December 14-16, 2007)

Children have always presented a paradox: time and energy, devotion and discipline, joy and grief, heartache and headache, money and still more money. And the writing of the history of children also presents its dilemmas—how to portray and respect a generation not only through traditional historical sources such as newspapers, magazines, government documents, educational reports, and census data but with an ear for children's own voices and an eye for particular young vantage points to capture and paint a true portrait of children's historical lives.

Children often have a skewed sense of chronology—certainly the days march on, but the order is easily mixed up. Linear time gets slightly out of order, becoming circles and spirals. (Swings. Teeter-totters. Merry-go-rounds.) Children crave a rhythm of repetition, routine, and pattern, yet

John [nickname Jack], Martha [Payne], Lawrence [nickname Corky], and William Smith in front of their home in northeast Iowa. Courtesy of Martha Payne.

they also yearn for the height of holidays and crazy celebration, especially Christmastime. (Presents. Gifts. Rewards.) Children can have surprisingly single-minded and devoted focus to their tasks when motivated, yet free play must necessarily remain part of their lives for emotional and moral development. (Baseball. Tag. Hide and seek.) Playing not only encourages the imagination but provides an outlet to relieve stresses. (Kick the can. Cops and robbers. War games.) This wish for fun is a deep human need, not easily or wisely suppressed even in times of war. (Dolls. Bikes. Tea sets. Guns.) Children also respond particularly and easily to the verbal story along with the love of a pun or rhyme that delights and persists within the memory. (Sing-alongs. Radio shows. Comic books.) Children also crave attention—positive or negative. All of this I have tried to include and reflect upon within this history of the Second World War.

Think back to your own childhood. Who were the most important people in your young personal narrative? When were you born? Where did you attend school and how would you describe the experience? Who loved, encouraged, cared for, neglected, frightened, hurt, or taught you? What images are flashpoints, forever memorable? What has been lost? What has been distorted or exaggerated? What still seems hazy or mysterious? Where did you live? Where do you still long to be? Which foods do you crave? Where and when were you afraid? What gave you pride?

Whom did you respect? Whom did you hate and whom did you love? When did you leave home? How are you similar to other members of your generation? How have you changed? Why do we continue to refer back to our childhood in so many conscious and unconscious ways? Why?

With those questions in mind, I and other historians have searched for sources of information about children's actual lives during particular historical eras. Answers. Documents. Phrases. Images. Omissions. Myths. Truths. And still more questions. Startling discoveries and regular routines. Unique. Ordinary. Patterns. Whatever happened during our childhoods, good or bad, almost always stays with us deeply, consciously and unconsciously. Youth is by chance, yes, but childhood is important and forever.

As abstract as children's perceptions can be, children believe very deeply in concrete issues—definite ideas of right and wrong, black and white, us and them. The "other." A wartime era only intensifies these characteristics. Feeling is far more important than knowing. Events and spaces can be much larger than reality. How did this complete paradox of experience affect American children's perception of World War II? How did they become "the forgotten generation"?

Acknowledgments

At the entrance leading to the fountains of the World War II Memorial in Washington, D.C., the lead-colored panels lining the path demonstrate the varied stories of American citizens during this extensive world war. Six children appear among the numerous adults in these twenty-four memorial scenarios: a child listens to the Pearl Harbor news on the radio; a newsboy sells papers with the headline "Germany Declares War"; three children march in a parade, carrying flags and selling war bonds; and a boy celebrates V-J Day by proudly displaying his own American flag. Children always participated in a variety of daily activities and memorable events that composed the home front era, yet one must carefully observe the details of this almost forgotten generation's contributions to the Second World War. "This was a people's war," states the last memorial's inscription by Colonel Oveta Culp Hobby, "and everyone was in it."

As I stopped to read this last inscription by Colonel Hobby, my cell phone chirped with a text message from my teenage daughter: "In 24 hours you will be in Iowa." Today's communication technology offers immediacy perhaps not available in the 1940s, but the messages conveyed still reflect those sent in children's letters and V-mails from World War II in that no child ever wishes to be forgotten. Children of both generations have reminded their parents to please come home.

Writing thank-you notes as a child always seemed necessary but difficult. I wondered why, if my heartfelt praise was within my spoken words and visible actions, I still needed to write it down on a card and send it off in the mail. But I didn't want to face Mom's wrath and I did want more presents in the future, so I would eventually sit myself down and write the best that I could do in a limited space. As an adult, writing the "thank you's" for a book presents me with the same dilemma—how, in just a few pages, to express my sincere praise with exactly the right words.

Only with family can one learn love and compromise, challenges and smiles. I certainly want to thank Mom and Dad (Susan and Roger Ossian, who were born during World War II) for always believing in me as a potential writer since I announced at the age of ten that I wanted to write big

Harriet [Olson], Roger, and Kathleen [Means] Ossian, Winterset, Iowa, 1943. Roger is the author's father.

books some day, starting that day with my scrawled notes in a secretarial dictation tablet. My daughters Bailey, Nellie, and Brita have also taught me the deepest meaning of family while being relatively tolerant of my writing work. These three have always kept me grounded for over twenty years. They instantly insisted that their photo should also appear on this book's jacket because the knowledge I have gained as a mother has certainly enabled me to write a history of children.

This national study certainly would not have been possible without the generous research travel grants that I received from five institutions. I would like to thank (in the order that I visited) the Margaret Chase Smith Library in Skowhegan, Maine, in which I received the Ada E. Leeke

Research Fellowship. The staff, particularly Gregory Gallant, director; David Richards, assistant director; and Angie Stockwell, collection specialist, were exemplary hosts to a historian at the beginning of her project. Angie remains one of the fastest and sweetest e-mailers I know to this day. I also stayed at the local bed and breakfast called Helen's in which I was served the best bacon and eggs each morning of that research week. Later that year I also received the Larry J. Hackman Research Residency Program Grant for a week's research in Albany at the New York State Archives.

In addition, I was granted another week's research time with a travel grant from the American Heritage Center at the University of Wyoming in Laramie, and I also enjoyed my stay at the bed and breakfast called The Brick, particularly the homemade chocolate-mint brownies on my pillow each night. My fourth grant was The Jacob Rader Marcus Center Fellowship at the American Jewish Archives in Cincinnati, Ohio, which also provided a week's research in their beautifully decorated and wonderfully pleasant archive along with the kind support of Kevin Proffitt, senior archivist. I stayed that week at The Clifton House, another lovely bed and breakfast that served not only gourmet breakfasts but also wine and homemade bread for a late-afternoon happy hour. My fifth research trip was provided by a travel grant from the Franklin D. Roosevelt Library and Archives in Hyde Park, New York. There too I stayed in an exemplary bed and breakfast named Journey Inn with wonderfully generous breakfasts along with sage advice from the owners about navigating New York City's Macy Parade on Thanksgiving.

Every staff member at the University of Missouri Press helps create an incredibly supportive team as each consistently keeps a sense of humor as well as retaining the best of professionalism. How many writers can truly say they look forward to reading each e-mail from their press? I have had that good fortune.

My colleagues and friends along this research and writing journey have given not only their time but advice and good wishes as well. I would like to thank Dr. James Marten, history professor at Marquette University, for suggesting this project and believing that I could be the one to write it. I will always remember sitting on a campus bench during a Society for the History of Children and Youth Conference as Jim detailed what the book should contain. Doris Weatherford and Richard Lowitt offered grand support of my first published book and have continued to believe in me as a scholar. My friend Jeremy Johnston, a history professor at Northwestern College in Powell, encouraged me to add Wyoming to my research agenda and generously offered his home for a stay so I could visit the internment camp Heart Mountain. His young son had a terrible earache that last day of my visit, however, and so Jeremy drove out to the memorial site to provide direction but left me in the Wyoming plains alone with just a warning to watch out for the snakes.

Another "thank you" should go to Dr. Stan Deaton at the Georgia Historical Society who listened so attentively at the end of a long, hot NEH seminar day in Savannah as I explained what I hoped to do within this book if only I could find a publisher. My cousin Paul Norris joined me on the two New York research trips—giving that sweetly sarcastic support that only family can provide as he continues to insist that historians lead wonderfully extravagant, expense-account lives. On one trip, Paul did share his secret chocolate chip cookie recipe with me, which has earned more praise than my research. And certainly I need to thank my friends and colleagues at Des Moines Area Community College—Julie Simanski, Maria Cochran, Joanne Dudgeon, Jim Stick, Dennis Kellogg, Bradley Dyke, Michael Jury, Randy Jedele, John Liepa, Dick Wagner, Eden Pearson, Joe Danielson, Mary West, and Lauren Rice—who have always listened with mostly patience to my history tales and tribulations.

And my final "thank you" must go to Vince Payne, who somehow found his way back into my life, creating our "new beginning." He is the one who reads my manuscripts and my eyes, the one who attends to my words and my gestures, the one who somehow understands me. He once knew me as a teenager when I drove a '65 Chevy Biscayne and now loves me as a woman (who continues to drive a Chevrolet). And so, in the words of another Tracy Chapman song, Vince is now simply and profoundly "where all my journeys end."

The Forgotten Generation

If there must be trouble, let it be in my day, that my child may have peace.

—Thomas Paine, 1776

It is a war for a new world. A new world for our children and our children's children.

—Paul McNutt, War Manpower Commission, 1942

I think that maybe if women and children were in charge, we would get somewhere.

—James Thurber

Introduction

A Child's Perspective on World War II

War is rapidly changing our way of life. It is affecting every home and school, every child in every community.

—"Our Wartime Report on the Nation's Children," *Parents* (1943)

America is a nation at war. We and our children with us are drawn closer and closer to an unknown ordeal for which previous wars have left no patterns.

—Anna W. M. Wolf, *Our Children Face War* (1942)

World War II would impact a generation of children unlike any other experience in the twentieth century. From the days before Pearl Harbor, with quiet rumors of war, to the dramatic Sunday afternoon of December 7, 1941, to the continuing days and years of war work, to the news of the atomic bomb, and finally to war's end on V-J Day, World War II challenged and transformed America's children. Two days after the attack on Pearl Harbor, President Franklin D. Roosevelt addressed the American people by radio: "We are all in it together—all the way. Every single man, woman, and child is a partner in the most tremendous undertaking of our American history." That phrase—"every single man, woman, and child"—echoed throughout the home front years.

The war years required work and sacrifice from every citizen. The conflict threatened and intensified every dimension of children's lives: family, school, play, work, and home. Children listened for news of Pearl Harbor over the radio, labored in munitions factories, harvested crops on the farm

A Kiwanis photograph of three female members of the House of Representatives in an aluminum scrap drive, with two Boy Scouts on the truck. July 1941. Courtesy of the Margaret Chase Smith Library.

front, saved money for war bonds, planted and weeded victory gardens, collected tin cans and newspapers for community scrap drives, stood in line for family ration books, watched enlisted men leave from train depots and bus stations, worried about soldiers' and sailors' safety overseas, prayed during the D-Day invasion, mourned President Roosevelt's sudden death, breathed a sigh of relief on V-E Day, and celebrated wildly on

V-J Day. Although children's experiences and perspectives differed from their parents', adults never sheltered them from the experiences of the home front but rather encouraged patriotism and a strong wartime work ethic. Every man, woman, and child would become very much involved in the work of fighting the Second World War.

Pearl Harbor was struck during an almost Christmastime—a holiday period of hopeful childhood dreams and wishes for the future. On that Sunday afternoon and evening of December 7, solemn adults suddenly were glued to their radios, whether at home or in the car, listening to war news, and children wondered and worried how this exciting and frightening talk of war might affect their lives. That Sunday at home and Monday at school disturbed many young people, both emotionally and physically.

Although the war seemed and remained physically remote for Americans, the culture of war propaganda and mobilization engulfed even children from the very beginning. Schools responded in January 1942 with a federal campaign titled "Schools for War," jointly sponsored by the Treasury Department, the Office of Education, and the National Commission on Children in Wartime, which coordinated children's war activities, especially bond drives, in all public schools. Teachers and parents encouraged students to behave as "good American citizens" and developed the "V for Victory" motto—"Sa**V**e, Ser**V**e, Conser**V**e." The government continued to bring the war into the classroom with revised textbooks and competitive contests for war bonds, and by the end of the war the nation's schoolchildren had contributed more than two billion dollars of their pennies and nickels to war bond sales. One cartoon caption summed up the propaganda: "I'm too little to fight . . . but I do buy bonds."

The United States certainly needed good, productive citizens to contribute food, munitions, and other materials to the war effort, and children (birth to sixteen years) composed almost a third of the American population, approximately 38 million of the 131 million citizens listed in the 1940 census. Americans raised homegrown food as one wartime solution, and each year "victory gardeners" produced approximately 8 million tons of food valued at half a million dollars in America's cities, suburbs, small towns, and farms. Ordinarily adults prepared and planted the family plots while the children received the weeding assignment. Still, children created their own gardens with some adult supervision in the 4-H Victory Garden program and the school-sponsored Junior Victory Gardeners. One mid-sized city campaign boasted 2,100 children who harvested 11,500 bushels of food in 1942.

Another war need was raw materials. The scrap drives for iron, paper, rubber, tin, kitchen fats, and milkweed pods thrived and survived because of energetic children who knew their neighborhoods intimately and scoured unusual places for scrap materials. As young scrappers, children often maintained the necessary determination to make community contributions successful, becoming the true heroes of the scrap drives. Formal clubs such as the Boy Scouts, Camp Fire Girls, 4-H, and Future Farmers of America (FFA) as well as informal neighborhood groups organized quasi-military units in which children could earn service rank and insignia, and the U.S. Office of War Information created a cartoon character, Kid Salvage, to support the war effort. The *Saturday Evening Post* proclaimed this salvage army of schoolchildren "the 30,000,000 soldiers for our New Third Front," and most adults believed children's efforts were necessary for wartime mobilization and motivation. As the historian Jordan Braverman has observed, "They supplied the earnestness that might have been lacking in their elders; they, at least, were not guilty of complacency." Although the children's voluntary efforts were admirable, the historian Marc Miller raises an important point: "The question arises why in the midst of an extremely popular war, this nation went to such lengths to indoctrinate its own children."[1]

Scrap drives and victory gardens remained volunteer opportunities, but most children's war efforts centered on their labor on family farms and local factories. On the farms, boys and girls worked increasingly longer hours with greater responsibilities, taking time from school and risking injury from machines, but parents and government officials deemed this idea of "little adults" acceptable for the all-out production demands of the farm front that was experiencing a desperate labor shortage. Urban children also participated in a federal program titled the Victory Farm Volunteers, which enlisted tens of thousands of young teenagers to participate in "day haul" programs to help local farmers with planting and harvesting. In some states during the war, rural and urban youth represented half of the additional agricultural labor needed on the farm front.

Although Rosie the Riveter remains the dominant image of the changing factory workforce, teenagers actually provided much of the dramatically increased demand for labor during the war years. By 1944, national school enrollment of fifteen- to eighteen-year-olds fell by 24 percent while the number of employed teenagers increased by more than 200 percent. Workloads as well as accident rates escalated for children, and other issues such as "door key" children and juvenile delinquency emerged because of the emphasis on mothers' war work. Teenagers' employment met with mixed community emotions of pride and concern: the war not only rekindled patriotism but resurrected the old debate between the traditional work ethic and the modern value of education as educators worried about increasing numbers of high school dropouts.

War may have provided economic opportunities for minors, but the challenges of a wartime economy also presented harsh lessons in discrimination. When President Roosevelt signed Executive Order 9066 in February 1942, the federal government forced more than 110,000 Japanese American men, women, and children to abandon homes, farms, and businesses and relocate to ten internment camps scattered throughout the western states. These second-generation Nisei, many of whom were children, had been born in the United States as citizens but were now denied their constitutional rights. Instead they experienced more than 900 days of overcrowding, boredom, and hard work. The younger children, along with their parents, endured cramped communal quarters surrounded by barbed-wire fences and guard towers. Teenagers and young adults could separate from their imprisoned families only by college enrollment, farm employment, or military enlistment.

Other American children, especially African Americans in the South, became part of the mass migration north and west to industrial cities for war jobs, yet these children still faced a segregated United States, a confusing world of inspiring rhetoric and challenging circumstances. Cities like Detroit, with its immense war plants, were not prepared for the influx and relocation of new defense workers, especially parents with dependent children. Schools quickly became overcrowded, housing remained substandard, and local residents maintained hostile attitudes and practices.

Despite the world's conflicts, children found time to play as children have always done. But during these years they mostly played war—from impromptu neighborhood battles attacking Hitler's Nazis to board games bombing the Japanese. Although commercial toys and games were few due to the rationing of materials, both boys' and girls' playtimes often emphasized militaristic themes. Also during their free time, children wrote letters to enlisted men, trying to relate their own activities and express their emotions. One little girl from Detroit exchanged letters with General Dwight D. Eisenhower throughout the war, saying that she had adopted him and prayed for his safety. "Ike" often referred to her as "my little godmother," refusing to travel without the lucky coins she had sent him. Another form of children's recreation included Saturday matinees of newsreels and war films, which both fascinated and horrified children as they gazed for hours at the depiction of war heroes and internalized the constant military bombardment. As the historian Stephen Ambrose noted, "When I was in grade school, World War II dominated my life." He remembered going with his brothers Harry and Bill to the movies three times a week to see films he later described as "stinkers and clinkers," but he vividly recalled the newsreels of fighting in North Africa, Europe, and

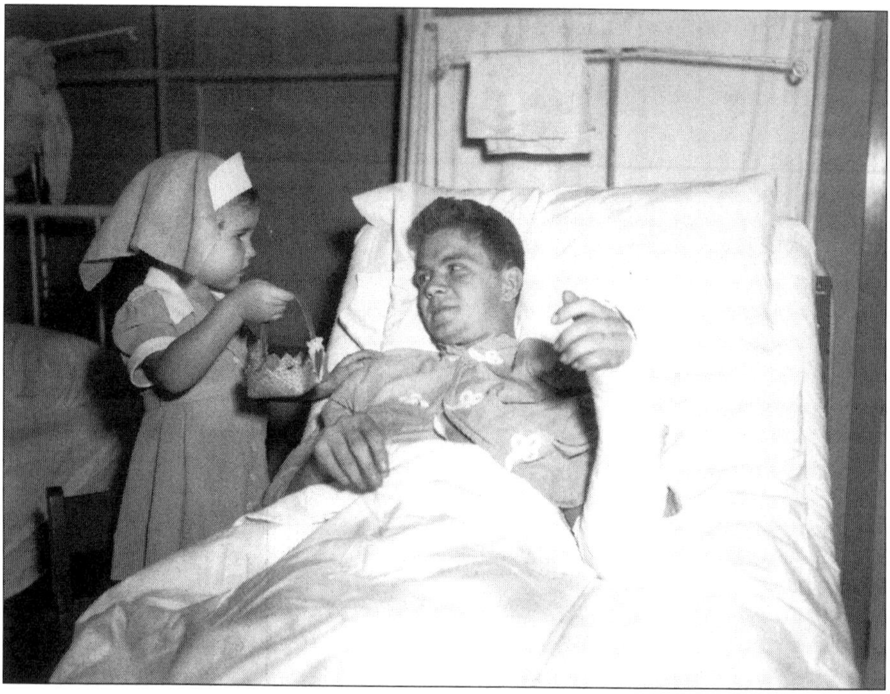

A little girl in a veterans' hospital. Courtesy of the University of Hawaii Archives.

the Pacific. "We played at war constantly," he said, "'Japs' vs. Marines, GIs vs. 'Krauts.'"[2]

Besides the movies and war games, Ambrose also remembered his mother's constant toil: working eight-hour factory days, gathering scrap, running a Cub Scout troop, and cooking hot meals every night. One of his sharpest wartime memories was the numerous tuna casseroles, along with his mother's constant admonishment: "Think of the poor starving children in Europe." American children did enjoy many material advantages compared to children living in war zones, but they nonetheless suffered tremendous losses—fathers never seen again, brothers perhaps maimed, cousins captured in POW camps, uncles lost to battle fatigue. And when President Roosevelt died in April 1945, young Americans lost the only president they had ever known.

Many children remembered a sadness and helplessness surrounding all their wartime grief, such as Mary Maloney's experience when she saw a woman sitting on a front porch with a small gold-star flag hanging in the window, indicating a loved one who had died in the war. Mary remembered, "I stopped and looked at her. I wanted to say I was sorry. I stood there for what seemed a long time and finally gave a little wave."[3] The grieving process was often silent, as sacrifices seemed necessary yet impossible for young children to comprehend. Although the devastation was far greater in Europe, Asia, and North Africa, World War II left children from the United States with too many scars and voids, too much violence and guilt, to ever be considered "the good war."

The war had begun shortly before Christmas and ended near the finish of the school year with V-E Day on May 8, 1945, and near the end of summer vacation with V-J Day on August 14, but children might not have paid much attention to these official days. In a child's eyes, the war's events could simply and suddenly be over on a very personal day. When Robert Moore enlisted for war duty, he left behind a wife and young daughter in their Midwestern town. When he returned to his family as a colonel sixteen months later, a photographer captured the intense moment at the hometown train depot in a Pulitzer Prize–winning photograph that appeared across the nation in *Life, Look, Time,* and *Newsweek.* All the faces are hidden, yet the emotion is dramatically apparent. This photo could have represented any one of thousands of American families: the war hero had suddenly become a family man again. As the uniformed father's arms tightly embraced and lifted his little girl, the mother held back and her hands covered her face in overwhelming disbelief and joy. In an uncropped version of the photo, a young nephew stands to the side, staring curiously. The Second World War was finally over.

The war held a variety of endings for America's home-front children along with lasting memories of pride and grief. The "forgotten generation" are those Americans squeezed between the "greatest generation" and the "baby boomers." These young, brave citizens were once partners on their nation's home front, where every single man, woman, and child contributed to the fighting of World War II.

1

Almost Christmastime

It was December, 1941, and Christmas was eighteen days off.

—Dorothy Baruch, *You, Your Children, and War* (1943)

Daddy, is this war?

—Colonel William C. Farnum's seven-year-old son, William Jr.
December 7, 1941: The Day the Japanese Attacked Pearl Harbor (1988)

The first Sunday of December 1941 began slowly in Hawaii, a morning of yellow sand, green fields, and blue ocean covered with a bright, peaceful sky and gentle breezes. The hills rolled, the mountains jagged, and the sea shimmered calmly. In military homes, beach shacks, and Sunday schools, little Hawaiian, Portuguese, Filipino, Chinese, Japanese, and *kamainas* children eased into a warm, lazy Sunday on the island of Oahu. This "Pacific Paradise" seemed remarkably safe and secure despite the world's storming war clouds. As one machinist remembered the quality of that morning, it seemed to have "a dream-inducing quietness." Another military man from Maine described his newfound paradise as "an island of dreams come true." But dreams do end, sometimes dramatically. And to Pearl Harbor, especially to the *keiki* (small children), came *auwe*: sudden surprise.[1]

The previous evening Japanese pilots had begun preparing for their own possible deaths during "Operation Hawaii." Plans had been excruciatingly complex and secret, but now in these hours before dawn, all that remained was contemplation and perhaps a little saki. Some of the pilots wrote farewell letters to their children; one prayed he could watch his baby daughter grow up. Captain Hara reminded the pilots to adhere strictly to the rules of warfare by striking only military objectives. In two waves at 5:30 a.m., 350 Japanese bombers and fighters lifted from their carriers and began flying over 200 miles above a silent ocean for Oahu's Pearl Harbor, homing in on the soft music of Honolulu's radio station KGMB. As Lieutenant Heita Muranaka headed for the island early that morning, he remembered hearing a sweet girl's voice over the radio singing the Japanese children's song, "Menkoi Kouma" ("Come on a Pony"). "Thinking about what would happen to such lovely children and what a change in their lives would occur only an hour and a half later," Muranaka recalled, "I couldn't listen to it any more and turned off the switch." As another pilot's plane finally approached the target, Lieutenant Yoshio Shiga distinctly remembered a particular image of Pearl Harbor: "The U.S. Fleet in the harbor looked so beautiful . . . just like toys on a child's floor—something that should not be attacked at all."[2]

Unaware of the approaching danger, the children of Hawaii began various early-morning activities that December day. The fifteen-year-old son of a commanding officer started reading his Superman comic book. A little girl, Roberta, watched her brother playing outside with his friend's wooden wagon. The three young children of army officer Harold Kay tried to play quietly in the living room as their parents argued once again about the safety of raising a family in Hawaii. Patricia and Eleanor Bellinger, ages fourteen and eleven, simply slept. Also snoozing sweetly in a bassinet was Staff Sergeant Stephen Koran's week-old baby girl. David Martin, now thirteen, waited while his military father made him a traditional morning cup of cocoa. Ten-year-olds Julia and Frances, twin daughters of General Howard C. Davidson, chased each other around their front lawn. After listening to music on the radio, six-year-old Dorinda Makanaonalani sat down to a family breakfast of Portuguese sausage with rice and eggs. And Charlie Jr., three-year-old son of Captain Charles Kengla, tried to wait patiently for the arrival of his Sunday School bus.[3]

Jimmy, the twelve-year-old son of Lieutenant Colonel Allen Haynes, stopped to chat with his mother in their kitchen a few minutes before 8 a.m. when terribly loud airplanes suddenly interrupted their conversation. He glanced out the window. "Mother," Jimmy declared, "those are Japanese planes." "Nonsense," she replied, until she too looked out the window to an awful discovery of the first wave of bombers.[4]

At 7:53, the commander of the naval base muttered when he spotted nine planes making forbidden maneuvers. "Those fools know," the commander barked, "there is a strict rule against making a right turn!" But his son, suddenly finished with his comic book, stared and pointed: "Look, red

A house hit during the Pearl Harbor attack. A child was killed inside the building. Photo courtesy of the University of Hawaii Archives.

circles on the wings!" At that very moment, Japanese commander Mitsuo Fuchida sent the prearranged attack signal: "Tora, tora, tora."[5]

When the first plane flew low over their house, little Roberta ran outside to get her brother and his friend out of the front yard. The Japanese plane then "splattered the sidewalk with machine gun bullets. The little wagon flew to pieces on the lawn."[6]

Officer Kay wondered why his children were making such a commotion, literally shaking the house right in the middle of this marital argument. When he stopped to quiet them, Kay then spotted the incoming planes. His wife Ann remarked as their debate quickly ended, "Well, it's war all right."[7]

After spotting the Japanese planes, Mrs. Bellinger ran to wake her daughters and rush them to the safety of the community shelter. Though still in her pajamas, teenage Patricia did grab her lipstick on the way. The sisters had played hide-and-seek in the shelter years before, but any games became quickly forgotten as other women and children, most of them still in their pajamas as well, began streaming into the Ford Island shelter. "They were white-faced," Mrs. Bellinger commented. "I kept thinking, what if this caves in and we're covered up. Will I be able to stand it?"[8]

Lieutenant Coe's three-year-old son did not wish to be cooped up in the Bellingers' shelter, and fearlessly, excitedly, he ran toward the sudden "Fourth of July fireworks." His desperate father remembered spending "a few breathless moments chasing him down while Japanese planes swooped and circled, machine-gunning the area." But the oldest citizen on Ford Island displayed little fear either. Eighty-year-old Lucy Mason, whose husband had died at Wounded Knee in 1890, refused "point-blank" to seek shelter. She had twelve canaries at home to worry about, and, Mrs. Mason insisted, those "young Japanese whippersnappers" did not scare her.[9]

The parents of the week-old baby along with the couple next door at first panicked but then ran to an abandoned concrete cesspool for protection. Recounted Flora Belle Koran, "So we—Marge, the baby and I, and her little Scottie dog—squeezed ourselves into a space about three feet by four feet and about two feet sunken under the ground. It was concrete but open at the top. We were under the banyan tree, and the trucks were parked there because banyan trees are so thick that from the air you cannot spot things underneath them. If one tracer bullet had hit those [trucks' gasoline tanks] . . . I didn't think about it at the time."[10]

Still waiting for his cocoa, David Martin pressed his face against the windowpane after hearing the first loud noise, which his father had assumed were planes arriving from California. "Dad," as David corrected him, "those planes have red circles on them."[11]

Julia and Frances, General Davidson's twin daughters, remained unaware of their immediate danger, joyfully picking up shiny pieces of shrapnel in the yard as planes strafed low over their heads. Their mom and dad raced into the yard and pulled the two girls inside to safety.[12]

When Dorinda Makanaonalani's family breakfast was interrupted by low-flying planes and loud explosions, her father dashed outside to see the source of the commotion, and she darted behind him. "We shielded our eyes from the early morning sun," Dorinda remembered, "and looked up into the orange-red emblem of the Rising Sun." Because of the low-flying attack pattern, she remembered seeing the Japanese pilots' goggles and hearing the "rat-tat-tat" of guns as incendiary bullets ripped into their kitchen, setting it ablaze.[13]

And little Charlie Jr., no longer diligently waiting for his Sunday School bus to arrive, ran impatiently into the house after the first commotion, shouting, "Daddy, there are planes and they go up and come down and they drop round things that go boom!"[14]

Years later Lieutenant Coe recalled the events during that first wave of Japanese planes from 7:53 to 8:35 a.m. "Officers and enlisted men were making a beeline to their stations," Coe remembered, "and civilians, women and children, were dashing for the safety of air raid shelters. There was also a hell of a noise overhead and out in the harbor. The sky was thick with planes, and machine guns were chattering madly." Another military man, Bill Caldwell, recalled fifty years later how the attack assaulted his senses: "the smells of planes and cars and people burning, the smell of gunfire, the sounds of attacking planes diving low, the indelible sound of bombs blowing up the place where you live and work and the air crews you live and work and play with."[15]

A local radio station blasted warnings to Hawaiian civilians: "The rising suns have been sighted on the planes' wings! Stay in the house! Get off the streets! Don't look up!" Another Honolulu station announced, "Ladies and gentlemen, this is an air raid. Take cover." After that brief statement, the station played "The Star Spangled Banner." Then silence.[16]

Bombs did not fall only on Pearl Harbor. A *Times* reporter later noted that "explosions wrenched the guts of Honolulu. All the way from Pacific Heights down to the center of town the planes soared, leaving a wake of destruction." Japanese pilots also sprayed bullets in the streets of Wahiawa, and planes rolled over Pearl City to drop bombs and torpedoes on "Battleship Row." After the initial forty minutes, an eerie quiet descended on the island, and everyone living in Hawaii that day would refer to this period between attack waves as "the lull."[17]

Navy man Leonard Webb remembered desperately trying to get his wife and baby to safety when the bullets first pummeled their neighborhood. As Webb helped his wife and daughter into their neighbor's car, she yelled to him that the baby girl needed diapers. "Bear in mind that this is Armageddon," he told his listener, "the end of the world, and my wife has me chasing diapers! And I went back for the diapers!"[18]

Pedestrians stood watching from Honolulu Hills as the heavy black smoke curled over Pearl Harbor. Soldiers quickly converted the city's largest high school, Farrington High, into a hospital, and medics brought dozens of the wounded men, severely burned from flaming oil and fiery bombs, to the other temporary hospitals at the Marine barracks and mess hall. One officer's sixteen-year-old daughter, though untrained in medicine, recorded names and comforted the dying sailors. "She knelt beside one man after another," noted the historian Gordon Prange, "cradling him in her arms like a sick child, easing his last moments from the deep well of compassion the Japanese bombs uncapped. As each one died, she gently laid him down, covered him reverently, and moved on to the next shattered patient."[19]

But this had only been the first blast of the Japanese attack. A second wave began hurling bullets, bombs, and torpedoes at the American fleet again at 8:55 until 9:55 a.m., an hour of intense pounding. During this strike, however, more U.S. sailors and soldiers angrily fired back. Civilians, however, possessed few if any defenses. Blake Clark, an English professor at the University of Hawaii, portrayed several scenes during the second wave. "Children were running up the street to where a part-Hawaiian man was holding a limp young girl in his arms," Clark recalled. "The family of five had been standing on the doorstep when the bomb fell. A piece of shrapnel had flown straight to the girl's heart. The man looked helplessly about him for a moment, then ran up the steps of his home and disappeared into the house with his dead daughter." Enemy fire killed another girl, a thirteen-year-old watching the attack from her front porch. Clark also remembered all the fleeing women and children in the middle of a close accident: "A plane swooped down, strafing. A machine-gun bullet went through the floor of the truck between Mrs. M and her eight-year-old boy." A veteran of the attack witnessed "one young mother running while trying to shelter two small heads, one in each arm, crying, 'My poor babies, my poor babies!'"[20]

Children lived not only in Hawaiian homes, but some boys had enlisted in the Navy and were stationed right in the midst of the attack. Just before the Arizona blew up, a fifteen-year-old seaman named Martin Matthews (who had managed to sign into the Navy with his father's cooperative deception) would forever remember the chaotic bloodshed of the harbor. "There were steel fragments in the air, fire, oil—God knows what all," Matthews recalled, "pieces of timber, pieces of the boat deck, canvas, and even pieces of bodies. I remember lots of steel and bodies coming down. I saw a thigh and leg; I saw fingers; I saw hands; I saw elbows and arms. It's far too much for a young boy of fifteen years to have seen . . ."[21]

Children witnessed other atrocious sights. At first Rose Wong, a teenager at the time, thought it fascinating to watch along with her brothers the Japanese planes flying back and forth over her Honolulu home. "We didn't know that we could've been killed," Rose explained. Her uncle ordered the children into the house shortly before a nearby bomb struck three teenage boys in a gruesome blast, and Rose remembered burning bits of their flesh and body parts dangling from the neighbors' trees.[22]

At 11:15 a.m., Hawaii's governor read a proclamation of emergency over the radio and then ordered the local radio stations to shut down, partly because their instructions were frightening rather than calming civilians but also so that radio signals would not act as a homing device for any additional Japanese bombers. Most military men and civilians now firmly believed an invasion was imminent. Martial law with its rules and constraints became effective that afternoon. Fear and panic deepened.[23]

Later that Sunday afternoon, Janet Yonamine Kishimori, a five-year-old Japanese-Hawaiian child, felt very lucky that she had survived the surprise attack, but she would be haunted by a future she could not have imagined. When the bombing began, her pastor had escorted the Sunday

School children to a safer building and then home after the second wave ceased. When she finally reached home, Janet found her mother hiding a picture of Emperor Hirohito so that officials would not consider their family disloyal. For the first time, Janet heard the word "war," and she remembered her mother's terrified look as if "monsters" had begun attacking the world.[24]

Some civilians had immediately sought shelter, and others continued to gather together throughout the day. Parents carried dozens of children to Hemingway Hall at the University of Hawaii where those too young to understand played with toys on the floor as dozens of enemy planes roared overhead. One cave offered cover to four hundred women and children; another dugout protected almost three hundred civilians. By midday, some two hundred women and children had crowded the Bellingers' Ford Island shelter. After a number of homes were destroyed, some mothers simply held their children close and dashed to the hills to find hoped-for safety, and dozens of families drove their cars into the sugar cane fields to hide but also to watch the attack above Pearl Harbor.[25]

The Marines' mess hall and barracks soon filled with hundreds of burn victims from the harbor's oil fires. "Men, women, and children were crying," one soldier reported. A nurse would always remember the chaos of the makeshift hospital: "People without arms or legs, many bleeding profusely, injured children, people paralyzed were piled on the beds, tables, floors, and in the halls." Many uninjured civilians found their way to the hospital and donated much-needed blood. Another nurse recalled that after donating blood, four girls stayed to wash medical tubing—describing the task as "the dirtiest, smelliest, meanest of all laboratory jobs. They worked hard and stayed at it as long as anyone." Everyone, young and old, seemed to be chanting the same refrain that terrifying afternoon: "I want to do something."[26]

The news of Pearl Harbor traveled quickly over the Pacific to the mainland. A Navy man home on a two-day leave in Keokuk, Iowa, recalled that particular afternoon of December 7 as "a beautiful day." "As we're going through Cedar Rapids, Iowa," Lewis Walker began, "we saw newsboys on the corners holding up papers yelling, 'Extra! Extra!' My dad, who was driving, stopped the car and bought a paper. The headline said 'Japanese Bomb Pearl Harbor.'" A newspaper boy in Battle Creek, Michigan, sold so many "extras" in an hour that afternoon he could later purchase a new bicycle, a valuable and rare item during wartime.[27]

Almost all Americans seemed stunned at the first news of Pearl Harbor. Alice Reid, a Southern black girl, remembered sitting on the family's sunny porch steps with her dog Mickey when she saw her neighbor, Mr.

Collins, running up the street. "'They bombin' Pearl Harbor! Get your radio on!' he shouted. We just gawked. 'It's a war!' a man said to two others. I still remember the glint in his eye. War. What was a war for? Why were these grown-ups so excited?" Still, Alice's mother insisted that her family finish their Sunday dinner together. "Years later, I idly asked her why she was so cross that afternoon. She said that she wasn't angry, she just knew that things were going to change. Everything did." Another slightly older girl, Amy Estes, also worried about her parents. "The crash of the dish my mother dropped," as Amy recalled, "made me listen [to the radio] and hear what was being said. I'll never forget the look on my parents' faces."[28]

Children worried not only about their parents but also about their family's military men. What would happen now? June Skelton Dickerson, a ten-year-old living in Wisconsin at the time, had just finished ice skating when she heard the news from her father, seated by the radio and listening intently. "He finally told me," June recalled, "the Japanese had attacked Pearl Harbor and the ship my brother was on, the *West Virginia*, had been bombed and sunk. We had no word about my brother Dean for several weeks. Then we heard he had been injured slightly but was safe. He spent the entire war in the Pacific and came home only after the war was over."[29]

The war news left most children simply confused and frightened for their immediate future. When her minister announced news of the attack in church, Hope Shrock recalled, "Being not quite four-years-old I did not understand what war was, but I knew it must be something bad because all the grown-ups were upset, some even started crying. I was afraid of this unknown monster, and I was glad mom was there." Pat Vang, who also lived in the Midwest, where her father ran a grocery store, heard the radio bulletin with her father. "I asked him what it meant and he said, 'War, little girl, war with the Japanese.'" As Pat later explained, "I was nine and it was a much more innocent world than we have today. I had never known war so I asked, 'Is it real bad, Daddy?' He looked so sad, this old veteran of World War I, and he said, 'Yes, baby, very, very bad. A lot of good men will die. That is what war is.'"[30]

Other men of that generation could only remember the awful trenches of the Great War rather than predicting any future triumphs in this emerging conflict. A feisty fourteen-year-old boy from Schoolcraft, Michigan, remembered announcing to his parents: "No one would want a war, but now that is has started, let's give 'em hell!" His father had tried to enlist in the First World War and now seemed much more bitter and far less enthusiastic. "Give 'em hell? Let's see what you say when they start bringing home the dead!"[31]

Another fourteen-year-old believed that "the Victory girl grew up in a hurry." "What I feel most about the war," this now-grown woman told Studs Terkel for his oral history *The Good War*, "it disrupted my family. That really chokes me up, makes me feel very sad that I lost that. On December 6, 1941, I was playing with paper dolls: Deanna Durbin, Sonja Henie. I had a Shirley Temple doll that I cherished. After Pearl Harbor, I never played with dolls again." Fifteen-year-old Vesta Lou Hubbard remembered asking her father about the attack: "What does it mean?" Her father replied with just one word, "War."[32]

A little boy who would turn nine a few days after Christmas distinctly remembered hearing the news of Pearl Harbor over the radio. "Even at my age, I sensed that this was different from the movies. This would touch us personally—for real. Christmas 1941 was not the same!" A boy named Forest Meek recalled his family "clustered around our big Montgomery Ward Airline console radio" as they waited for *The Shadow* to begin at 5:30 p.m. Forest had had a day of sledding and was now tiredly but anxiously awaiting their early evening drama. Suddenly a serious-sounding announcer broke into the program: "We interrupt this program to inform you that the Japanese have launched an air attack upon our military forces at Pearl Harbor." As Forest later recalled, "What kid in the eighth grade knew where Pearl Harbor was?"[33]

A "going on ten" boy, Theodore Ho, began making his way to Sunday School class at the Salvation Army mission on the Hawaiian island of Oahu when the attack began. Theodore remembered the bright blue Hawaiian skies quickly turning to clouds of black smoke as he described a sense of almost detached wonder. "We stood in the lane in front of our house and watched the anti-aircraft shells explode in the sky trying to down Japanese planes," Theodore began. "We could see the rising sun insignia on their wing tips. Also, we watched in fascination as several Army Air Force P–40 Warhawk airplanes engaged several Japanese Zeros in dogfights." But later that night in the midst of martial law, this little boy had other thoughts: "The reality of war sank in as the sun set."[34]

As the Hawaiian night darkened, deeper fears arose. Would any more waves of bombers attack? Would the Japanese invade the island? Rumors flew quickly, soldiers and sailors became increasingly trigger-happy, and tracer bullets illuminated an otherwise black sky. That night, and for many nights to come, Hawaii remained totally blacked out. "Many of the women lost control of themselves and their children," as historian Gordon Prange described the scene, "screaming, crying, and mumbling prayers." Others remained stoic, but some women experienced an overwhelming urge to smoke despite the sudden and complete blackout. "That night," Navy wife Eliza Isaacs declared, "was the longest I ever put in." Little

Toshi Oda, age two, seemed to symbolize that night's mix of emotions after the morning bombing of Pearl Harbor as Toshi sadly and desperately clutched all that remained of her once-pretty doll. No one knew what the following morning might bring.[35]

On the morning after the Japanese attack on Pearl Harbor, President Roosevelt stood alone at the podium to address Congress, reading from a black loose-leaf notebook that looked like a schoolchild's. The president began his declaration of war with the now famous words: "Yesterday, December 7, 1941—a date which will live in infamy—the United States of America was suddenly and deliberately attacked."[36]

After listening to the declaration on the radio, a number of children across the country wrote directly to President Roosevelt, describing their concern about war and restating their belief in democracy. The next day a sixth-grade teacher at John Barry School in Philadelphia sent sixty-two student letters to the White House, and four of these letters particularly captured the children's collective sentiments.

Arthur McLane: "I'm with you all the way in this war for freedom and Democracy. I do not like war as I'm sure you don't neither. But if we have to fight I'm willing to help all I can. Japan started this war and we'll end it in victory."

Douglas M. Jacobs: "I think it was terribal of such a nation like Japan to do what had happened. On Sunday 12/7/41. To bomb Islands that were under our protection. We have got into this war but with the help of Almighty God we will win this war. 'I Hope.' P.S. 'Keep on Rolling. Keep on Flying. Keep Democracy from Dying. Buy Defense Bonds.'"

Delores Davis: "When my father told me that United States was in war, I was very surprised. Just think we were all free, until a thing like this had to happen. We can never tell what may happen to us. But I will do my part by saving up my money and buying defense saving bonds and stamps, and be a good citizen and help America."

Jean Batchelor: "We are in war now. We all got a task to do. Japan attacked some Island near the coast and bombed them. . . . We are fighting for Peace and Democrasie. P.S. I will never forget Dec. 7, 1941."[37]

Another teacher from Barrett Junior High School in Philadelphia sent 102 student letters to the president. "These letters have not been corrected," the teacher explained, "and I'm afraid the many errors prove that. They are the result of a class lesson on national unity. The boys and girls wanted to show they supported you one hundred per cent. They wanted to give expression never to yield to aggression." Most of the students' letters offered strong yet childlike desires to "do my duty as an American citizen."

Ben Davis: "If I were to tell you what I think of Japan, it would take me all day, but I will do all I can to help in National Defence."

Juanita Blount: "The Japanese certainly gave us a stab in the back. Cheer up 'cause we are going to pull that knife out. I will do all I can to defend our country."

Naomi Gary: "Sunday Dec. 7, 1941 is a date of memory in my heart which shall never die that Japan struck our country behind our backs."[38]

With the United States now officially at war, martial law continued in the Hawaiian Islands for more than a year until March 1943. As one congressional representative described the region by the end of the war, "The tourists' paradise was bombed into martial frenzy." Life changed on the islands: regulations, shortages, long lines, barbed wire, blackouts, and curfews became routine. The military issued gas masks to all civilians, and the smaller children's masks came in brown canvas bags for carrying to classrooms once schools resumed session. Even babies needed gas masks now. Still, military shortages occurred, and seven hundred students at the Royal School had to make do with emergency masks that offered only

Boy Scouts receiving an award for assistance. Courtesy of the University of Hawaii Archives.

"some measure of protection." Honolulu was the first and only American city to be bombed during World War II, and for weeks Pearl Harbor reeked of black oil, charred wood, and bloated dead bodies. As one Hawaiian civilian described their new world, the days were now completely *kapakahi*, which in Hawaiian means "what has happened to our way of life?"[39]

Hawaii's civilians worked to recover, reorder, and readjust to their new wartime lives. Honolulu's Boy Scouts proved exceptionally steady and useful in the weeks following the attack by giving first aid, directing ambulances, carrying messages, putting out fires, serving food, aiding evacuees, and looking after small children. A *Life* reporter described many of the civilians' new energy: "Its people gave blood, rolled bandages, dug trenches and shelters, and surrendered most of their civil rights under martial law. In the confusion of the first few war weeks, some of their energy was misdirected. But now they have settled into a normal routine of living, broken only when someone stubs a toe in the blackout or catches a bathing suit in the barbed wire of a beach barricade."[40]

Two days after the declaration of war, President Roosevelt spoke to the country by radio, reminding all Americans of the treacherous path ahead. "It will not only be a long war," the president explained, "it will be a hard war." But he also offered a note of hope for the continuing struggle. "We are now in the midst of a war," Roosevelt concluded, "not for conquest, not for vengeance, but for a world in which this nation, and all that this nation represents, will be safe for our children."[41]

Near Christmas, hundreds of Navy women and children evacuees of Oahu arrived in San Francisco. Unfortunately, the military had given the mothers little notice before issuing orders to travel more than two thousand miles, leaving no time for them to pack more than a few blankets for the babies. The youngest of the evacuees was four-week-old Ellen Koran. Though worried about her baby's serious cold, Ellen's mother always remembered the quiet bravery of a little boy on that evacuation ship, burned so severely he was blinded. As another young family disembarked from the ship, the mother held her two-year-old boy by one hand and her four-year-old with the other. The older brother's little suitcase read "Little Country Doctor," while beside him real doctors and nurses helped injured sailors and soldiers returning to the mainland. One twelve-year-old boy, trying to act courageous far beyond his years, proclaimed, "I didn't want to come here. I wanted to stay in Honolulu and fight." Another tough young teenager spoke for his five siblings: "We want to go back and clean up on those guys. Maybe pretty soon we'll be big enough."[42]

Three little girls, Noel, Merrily, and Gerta (two aptly named for the Christmas season), also arrived with the Hawaiian group. These young

Mothers receiving orders to sail to the States. Courtesy of the University of Hawaii Archives.

sisters had worried about war but continued to fret about Christmas, asking their parents if Santa Claus would still be able to deliver their gifts. "I had tried to prepare them," their mother explained to a reporter, "by telling them that because of 'conditions' Santa couldn't get to Hawaii on his surfboard—that's how he gets there, you know."[43]

At the White House that Christmas season, no one hung stockings because no grandchildren were expected due to wartime conditions. Mrs. Roosevelt thought it seemed a bit sad without the homey decorations of children, and she encouraged parents to remember to tell their children of Santa Claus, "the whitest lie of them all." "Why not let them have the joy of believing," the First Lady said, "that Santa Claus does come to all children and that he is such a jolly old saint?"[44]

Santa became even busier for the rest of the season with the added government duty of selling defense bonds. According to the Treasury Department, a book of defense stamps best expressed the spirit of the season, and its advertisements encouraged parents to buy bonds for Christmas presents as "a more significant gift" rather than "trinkets and baubles and toys." Federal Christmas cards with Santa's image also promoted defense stamps that year, but many adults, however, tried to recreate Santa as a reassuring symbol of peace. "Santa wasn't worried much about the war bulletins," a *Des Moines Register* editorial explained. "Santa is very old, and he's been through all this many times. You can't bomb out Santa Claus."[45]

Another "apple-cheeked and twinkle-eyed" man who was not afraid of Japanese bombs was Britain's prime minister, Winston Churchill. Leaving the wartime conditions of London, Churchill arrived in Washington, D.C., to form alliance war plans and boost American morale. When he offered his prayerful inspiration that Christmas Eve from the White House lawn, he gathered together not only the holiday crowd but their spirit of resolve. Addressing the cause of children, Churchill said, "Therefore, we may cast aside for this night at least, the cares and dangers which beset us and make for the children an evening of happiness in a world of storm."[46]

The prime minister concluded his pronouncement to the American people that holiday evening. "Let the children have their night of fun and laughter," advised Churchill. "Let the gifts of Father Christmas delight in their play. Let us grown-ups share to the full in their unstinted pleasures before we turn again to the stern task and the formidable years that lie before us, resolved that, by our sacrifice and daring, these same children shall not be robbed of their inheritance nor denied their right to live in a free and decent world."[47]

Public moments of great words and inspiration were noteworthy during that almost Christmastime of 1941, yet far more private moments of quiet and mourning took place, such as an anxious Christmas Eve scene in Atlanta, Georgia. A young Western Union messenger boy trudged up the steps of St. Joseph's Infirmary that evening, just as another nervous delivery boy had brought a telegram on December 7 announcing the death of a nurse's brother from the Pearl Harbor attack. This second tragic telegram on Christmas Eve was intended for another nurse, also informing her of a brother's death. For not only the nurses that sad holiday night but for the interns, nuns, cooks, and elevator boys, the Second World War had become very lonely and very personal.[48]

On that same evening in Hawaii, Sabilla Schmid decided "to store one final memory of Pearl Harbor" before she and her son boarded the ship the next morning to California. "On Christmas Eve, at night, it was moonlight," Sabilla reminisced. "And my neighbor and her daughter and my son and I, we went out and sat on the lawn. And we sang 'Silent Night, Holy Night,' and my son played the accordion. Nobody would have ever known there was anybody in any of those houses around there because nobody could turn their lights on." Then came a moment that lived on poignantly for Sabilla: "But after we got through, you should have heard the clapping coming from everybody's windows . . . You just don't know what we went through. Nobody will ever know."[49]

2

Schools for War

Education for Victory till Victory is Won.

—John W. Studebaker, U.S. Commissioner of Education (1942)

If we can afford war, we can also afford education.

—Henry Ford (1942)

"I am speaking to you tonight," Eleanor Roosevelt began her broadcast on the evening of December 7, 1941, "at a very serious moment in our history." Mrs. Roosevelt addressed her remarks to "the young people of the nation" as she called Americans to "National Faith." "You are going to have a great opportunity," the first lady continued. "There will be high moments in which your strength and your ability will be tested. I have faith in you. I feel as though I were standing upon a rock, and that is my faith in my fellow citizens."[1] So began the journey for America's young citizens as their strengths and abilities would be tested by the stresses and deprivations of the Second World War, and schoolchildren in particular would prove to be a rock of ability, strength, and determination.

After the anxiety of that startling Sunday, most children probably looked forward to their routine of school on Monday morning. Although no one knew what the future would hold, most Americans began to realize that their hours and their days for years to come would be devoted to war work. Walking to the school bus stop early that Monday morning, a twelve-year-old Louisiana boy named Richard Young watched his uncle, a Great War veteran, approach holding a copy of the *New Orleans Times-Picayune*. "Boy, we are in trouble now," his uncle grumbled. Those words and his uncle's war stories from earlier years would leave a serious im-

A wartime classroom with children studying Africa on the globe. Courtesy of the State Historical Society of Iowa Archives.

pression on Richard that would echo throughout the war years. "When the schools opened on Monday, December 8," declared A War Policy for American Schools, "they had one dominant purpose—complete, intelligent and enthusiastic cooperation in the war."[2]

As President Roosevelt's address to Congress was broadcast across America that morning, many schoolchildren sat restlessly at their desks or perched uncomfortably in gymnasiums as their teachers insisted they listen to this historic moment. On her own initiative, Matilda Mally brought a radio into her elementary classroom in Des Moines, Iowa, and reported that as her students listened, their expressions displayed "intense interest." In Long Beach, California, sixth-grader Raymond Parker remembered his teacher also bringing a radio "so we could hear President Roosevelt's historic 'Day of Infamy' speech, as he declared war on the Japanese empire."[3]

Most children of school age grasped the importance of the sudden anxiety surrounding them, and a child psychologist warned caregivers that young children might be affected very personally "by displays of adult emotions such as they had rarely experienced." Radio announcements punctuated with adult voices sharp with fear left too many children's questions unanswered. In those immediate days after Pearl Harbor, a Midwestern rural schoolteacher named Deloris Murphy also worried about her young students' recent obsession with war. "All my students talk about is the war," Murphy noted ruefully. "They think we must fight the Japs and that we'll be fighting Hitler soon."[4]

The anthropologist Margaret Mead explained to adult audiences that "war need not mar our children." And Mead also asked the question that almost any parent or educator considered: "Can we protect our children in wartime?" As a realistic observer of the world, her professional answer was probably one most caregivers did not wish to hear at the time. "In the bottom of their hearts most Americans believe that we cannot," Mead confessed, "that we are condemned to seeing a whole generation of little children marred by war."[5]

An educator named Luchen Aigner wrote in an essay titled "The Impress of War on the Child's Mind," an acknowledgment that any attempt after Pearl Harbor to keep the war out of schools would probably be fruitless. "Before that parents and educators largely agreed that the war should be kept out of the classroom," Aigner noted. "Now they feel the school must do what it can to guide the children in assimilating their war impressions in a healthy way."[6] Like it or not, the war had entered the American classroom.

Official agencies added comments that proved to be more reassuring than realistic. Only days after the Pearl Harbor attack, the Office of Civilian Defense (OCD) advised adults to "skip war talk with children" and urged American parents, with a luxury that others in war-torn regions of the world simply did not have, to "direct their energies into useful defense tasks such as knitting and dishwashing." "Any chore," the OCD advised, "that helps make a child self-sufficient is good defense." Keeping busy soon became an antidote for war nerves in young and old alike, and most adults believed that children should be included in the home front war effort. "We have begun the work," as President Roosevelt told America's teachers. "Our children must carry it through."[7] Teachers understood their newly appointed role: to support the government's effort to wage war while simultaneously encouraging young students' wartime participation.

Would the United States face the same physical dangers as London did during the Blitz air raids in the autumn of 1940? In December 1941 no one in America seemed to know for sure, yet school officials on both coasts remained unprepared, with no coherent plan, unlike the mass evacuation

Girls with gas masks. Courtesy of the University of Hawaii Archives.

of England's urban children that had begun as early as September 1939. Within a week after Pearl Harbor, however, the Office of Civilian Defense issued school air raid precautions with alarms, drills, and training. "We don't intend to be caught napping again—anywhere or anytime," proclaimed the OCD. Napping implied infancy or old age, and America must immediately regain its vigor and vigilance.[8]

In Washington, D.C., schoolchildren received identification tags similar to those used in England's evacuation. West Coast schools in particular prepared for air raids that never materialized, and a number of Los Angeles children carried bedrolls to their classrooms in the event of overnight bombing attacks or practiced sitting quietly in their hallways during air raid drills. Schoolchildren in New York City pasted paper to their windows to reduce the danger of flying glass in an air raid, and in Hawaii school children intently practiced adjusting their gas masks while studying other medical precautions.[9]

Shortly after Pearl Harbor, a concerned citizen wrote to the *Washington Post* to suggest an escalation of children's wartime participation, particularly in the educational realm. "This is a plea," the letter began, "for every school in the country to make its scholars, every one of them, feel they have a job and a necessary one in this defense program, that must start at once in the private as well as the public schools." The writer suggested that hours previously dedicated to sports should now be devoted to practical training in such skills as dousing incendiary bombs, learning first-aid techniques, and adjusting blackout curtains. "The schools should make every child feel he is a necessary part of the defense program," the writer concluded, "that he has a job in guarding his home and family."[10]

Although no Axis bombers circled eastern cities, the New York City school system tested an air raid procedure just days after the start of war and found it only produced mayhem. "Confusion marked the occasion," as the board of education president explained, "as school principals were puzzled as to the proper procedure. The warning sirens wailed at 8:40 a.m. just about the time most of the children were settling down in their classrooms." One school in Queens simply dismissed eleven hundred children and told them to return at 1 p.m. School officials had tried to implement precautions for the evacuation of children from a new instruction booklet titled "Air Raid Dangers to Schools" issued by the Board of Education's Committee on Civilian Defense in the Schools, although some emergency drills had turned dangerously and embarrassingly chaotic.[11]

School administrators, however, seriously embraced their new war roles. Within two weeks of the U.S. declaration of war, leading educators established a Wartime Commission within the Office of Education "to consider plans for the mobilization of American school resources to win the war." As one organizer emphasized to fellow educators, "Whether you like it or not, whether you wear a uniform or not, you're in the Army now. That—or a Nazi strait-jacket later."[12]

Although the war seemed remote for most Americans, the culture of war propaganda and mobilization engulfed children from the very beginning. Teachers and parents continuously encouraged students to behave as "good American citizens." Federal school officials responded in January 1942 with a nationwide campaign titled "Schools for War" to coordinate children's war activities in all public schools, urging each student in the United States "to intensify and unify its war services to SaVe Money to Buy War Bonds and Stamps, SerVe only days after the Pearl Harbor attack, SerVe its community and nation, as well as ConserVe materials of all kinds for the war effort." This "V for Victory" motto, as the new journal *Education for Victory* explained, succinctly reminded children of their new responsibilities: "SaVe, SerVe, ConserVe."[13]

When it began, the Schools for War program did not seem to trouble parents, teachers, or administrators that schools should now focus so much attention and energy on war tasks. The American system of education was difficult to measure during this or any other time due to its decentralization. Only later would a historian, reflecting on his own wartime childhood, note the "heavy doses of the patriotism and democratic ideology that prevailed on the home front."[14]

Official messages reinforced children's wartime roles without reservation. The National Education Association (NEA) published "What the Schools Should Teach in Wartime," and the Office of Education's Wartime Commission printed a "Handbook on Education and the War" and also created *Education for Victory,* which went to 60,000 educators twice a month throughout the four years of the war. As NEA executive secretary Dr. William Carr explained, "American education is not only essential to the American way of life but must play a crucial role in wartime." Writers at *Parents* magazine composed "Our Wartime Report on the Nation's Children" as a guide "to prepare boys and girls for the new roles they must fill in a wartime era." The report quoted Lieutenant General Brehon Somervell's new militaristic philosophy for all of America's schools: "Every classroom a citadel."[15]

With little apparent public ambivalence, school officials portrayed children's participation in the war as essential such as Virginia's school policy, which stated a goal for each student: "Your part in the fight for freedom." Or as the District of Columbia public schools representative declared in a paraphrase of Roosevelt, "Total war requires total effort. Every man, woman, and child has the patriotic duty to contribute to victory by rendering services or by making sacrifices. The schools are enlisted for the duration and for the long future."[16]

Public displays of patriotism by schoolchildren included parades and petitions. Three hundred elementary students joyfully marched to their North Hollywood school one April morning in 1942 to demonstrate their frugal patriotism. Their "war emergency game" included waving flags, singing songs, and beating drums. Walking to school for the duration of the war, the children proclaimed to their adult audience that they would save tires as well as build their health.[17]

In her book *Our Children Face War,* the child psychologist Anna Wolf expressed her belief that children wished to serve their country with ever increasing ideals of patriotism and citizenship. In order to assimilate vast numbers of new immigrants at the turn of the century, American schools had taught particularly nationalistic lessons, and World War II added to this patriotic volume. "Schools in America have danced to different drummers during their long history," Patricia Albjerg Graham explains in *Schooling America,* and during World War II, "the principal purpose of schooling seemed to be teaching citizenship and developing habits of work appropriate for a democratic society."[18]

But young Americans' patriotism, officials agreed, should in no way resemble the organized pomp of the Hitler Youth organizations. The overriding principle of the "Schools for War" program was Americanism—to develop within young citizens a strong, unbreakable sense of patriotism. For instance, the Jewish community in New York City viewed these war years as a strong educational tool. Samuel Rosenman, president of New York's Jewish Education Committee, believed that "the Jewish community owes it to America as well as to itself to implant the teachings and ideals of our faith in the hearts and minds of our children; for those teachings are a bulwark of the freedom and democracy we are fighting to preserve."[19]

Patriotic ceremonies sometimes elaborately staged such democratic beliefs. The Jewish children's magazine *World Over* described one such event when two thousand children from New York City's Jewish schools attended the second annual Children's Community Assembly in 1942 on George Washington's birthday. At the opening of the ceremony, Boy Scouts carried flags of the Allied nations as the audience sang "The Star Spangled Banner" and the *Hatikvah*. The students pledged to plant ten thousand trees in George Washington Forest in Palestine to honor both the Founding Father of the United States and the continued determination of the world's Jewish people. Five months after Pearl Harbor, in another New York City ceremony called "I Am an American Day," public and private school students collected more than 5 million signatures of New Yorkers who pledged to support the American home front war effort. Mayor La Guardia received these scrolls with the appropriate formality, noting the children's diligent work.[20]

Patriotic messages infused the schools, perhaps best illustrated by students' projects and plays. The Student War Council in Albany, New York, set as its initial goal participation by every high school student in the city, and the council's ten rules centered on curbing un-American materialism, requiring absolute cooperation with war aims, and asking all high school students to "give their time to the prosecution of the war." Other quasi-military organizations, such as a national project called Victory Corps, placed 6.5 million students from 28,000 high schools into war program roles, complete with militaristic caps and armbands. Encouraging local direction and democratic principles, the Victory Corps wanted youth to participate as "equal partners in the war effort."[21]

The Victory Publications Clearing House published four "playlets" by Bertha Brown of New York City for performance by schools in the service of patriotic education. Each of the four scripts cost a dime: "At Your Service, Men in Arms," "Waste Helps the Enemy," "The Extravagant Wilsons," and "Grandpappy Jones Helps Uncle Sam." The order form explained the particular wartime focus: "It is thought that through the use of this material the urgency and necessity of the various civilian war efforts can be driven home in a very pleasant and forceful manner."

Another series of plays published by Samuel French in 1941 sounded even more patriotic: "What Is America?: A Patriotic Playlet in One Act," "It Happened Next Tuesday: A Play of Americans for Americans," and "Youth and Uncle Sam: A Lively Comedy Drama of High School Life in One Act." In "Little New Citizen" (to be performed by five boys and five girls), an excerpt illustrates the patriotic flavor:

James: Joe wanted to have a club last month, but we didn't know what kind of club to have. Joe thought of calling it the Young Citizens' Club.

Rhoda: He said the sooner we begin to learn how good and great our country is, the better citizens we shall be when we grow up.

Louise: A lot of people have just moved in here from foreign countries, to work in the factories. Some of them are refugees from countries at war. Now they'll have boys and girls who'll be coming to this school.

(Maria is a refugee from "Dictoria.")

Maria (earnestly): Oh, in this kind country I wish to be a very good citizen. I wish to be a good American citizen right away. I think this "over here" is a very fine place!

All the others (in concert): So do we, Maria!

(The children line up, facing the audience, and Louise and Joe lead them in singing two stanzas of "America.")

What did America stand for in this war? What did democracy really mean? By March 1942, teachers could purchase booklets, motion pictures, slide films, lantern slides, transcriptions, and posters available from the National Association of Manufacturers. This School Patriotic Series included posters, one of them titled "Credo of an American Child": "I believe in what I can see with my eyes . . . what I can feel with my hands . . . what I hear with my ears . . . the people I know . . . I believe in America." These patriotic concerns were raised early on in this global conflict and persisted into the early postwar years. In February 1942 when the *Atlanta Constitution* sponsored a "Win Americanism Contest," the unanimous decision of the Atlanta Junior Chamber of Commerce for the theme of the contest was "Young Americans are Good Americans."[22]

This democratic force rolled across the states in waves throughout the war years from urban high schools to rural elementary schools as all schoolchildren strived to be "good Americans." Elois Anderson from Iowa wrote just such a theme in a poem for *Successful Farming* titled "The Voice of Young America":[23]

We're proud to be little Americans
In this land of the brave and free,
Where everyone's considered important,
Even little folk like You and Me!

Americanism emerged as the first component of the Schools for War "ABCs." The second component would be bonds. These war loans by

American citizens—young and old—to the government became expressions of democratic commitment translated into wartime participation. "I am 11 years and can't get in the Marines," explained one young boy from Royal Oak, Michigan, to President Roosevelt, "so I'm sending you $427.80 to help win the war. If you need any more just write to me." Teddy Burton picked such a large and unusual amount of money after listening to Roosevelt's budget speech suggesting that each American's share of the war was $427.80; children often translated such radio war appeals literally, such as in Los Angeles when Harry Beam's three children donated their entire savings from neighborhood chores—$1,012.50—to war bonds.[24]

Children's financial contributions not only served as markers of conscientious wartime participation but prompted guilt among adults about their possible lackluster participation. Smaller donations remained far more common for most children, and a great deal of media attention was paid to these contributions. One such example was the Boys' Athletic League's Penny Bank Brigade among New York City's West Side children, ages four and five. To make their transactions official and newsworthy, the boys broke their piggy banks in front of Postmaster Albert Goldman. Ten- to twelve-year-old members of the Victory Club at the Navajo Ordnance Depot also sold war bonds, a sentimental inspiration for adults to contribute even larger amounts of money to their government's war effort.[25]

Within a week after Pearl Harbor, New York City's superintendent of schools received an urgent request from the Junior Red Cross for "permission to enlist the financial support" of the city's million schoolchildren to create a $50 million national war fund. The junior division already numbered 9 million children nationally and hoped to strengthen its membership during the war years. "The purpose of enlisting the school children is not merely to get a certain amount of money," the Red Cross president promised, "but has the much larger purpose of making them realize that they are a real part of the war effort and are helping our armed forces. Never in all our history has there been a time of national needs such as this."[26]

The federal government followed suit in asking for money from the nation's schoolchildren—one dime a week per child on average—eventually totaling $2 billion of the total $131 billion collected in Series E bonds designed for citizen investments. Federal loan campaigns continued to make adjustments to encourage schoolchildren's participation. Shortly before V-E Day in 1945, an announcement appeared in newspapers across the country for the "Mighty 7th": "To permit school participation, the 7th War Loan starts May 14, ends June 30." Yet despite all the advertising and educational attempts, children (like many adults) probably found the idea of bonds rather abstract. As Robert Kirk explained in *Earning Their*

A girl with her winning bond poster. Courtesy of the University of Hawaii Archives.

Stripes, "American children equated war savings with war giving, particularly when bond redemption dates seemed hopelessly remote."[27] In other words, children's contributions of their nickels and dimes were even more generous since the children viewed them not as an investment but as a true gift to their government in time of need.

Often a more effective fund-raising tactic for both children and adults involved the direct connection of war donations with actual military items. For example, Stuart Scheftel, editor of *Young American* and founder of Young America Victory Clubs, created a two-day campaign where schoolchildren throughout the country collected $6,000 in pennies, nickels, and dimes, enough to purchase three new ambulances for the Allied forces. Nationally, children typically donated almost $50 million a month through their schools.[28]

Another marketing strategy targeted parental concerns, promoting the idea that war bonds purchased for children had peaceful purposes such as ensuring college educations. "You may wonder what this picture of a little girl is doing in an advertisement filled with guns and bayonets," one war bond ad began. "This little girl is nine. Ten years from today your $25 will pay her tuition for two weeks at almost any college you want to name."[29]

Still, some war bond marketing aimed directly at childish desires. Toy stores prepared "a new patriotic, three-dimensional playbook with twenty action-crammed pages! Plus a War Savings Stamp Book with a real ten cent stamp pasted in!" The ad copy promised, "It'll captivate every boy from four to fourteen!" This all-in-one playbook included illustrations of bombers, torpedoes, and saboteurs along with the twenty-six flags of the Allied nations.[30]

The war bond message was without discrimination. More than five hundred African American high schools adopted bond and stamp selling as part of the war program with art departments creating special war savings posters. In the Japanese American internment camp in Heart Mountain, Wyoming, the weekly newspaper created a cartoon character schoolboy who also regularly and enthusiastically donated to the war bond drives. And *World Over* created a Jewish cartoon character named Joey who dispensed wartime advice. At the end of May 1944, Joey's last caption of the school year noted, "Dear Kids, Don't forget to keep buying War Savings Stamps. See you in the fall."[31]

A poem by Atlanta fifth grader William Caldwell perhaps summed up this range of experience—from pride to fear to guilt—that schoolchildren felt as they were thrown into the midst of wartime financial participation:

Defense is very confusing to me,
We're just as busy as a bee
I think I should do my part
But I don't know where to start
People are building guns and tanks
Soldiers are marching in their ranks;
So I will keep the home flag flying
With defense stamps that I'm buying.[32]

The third component of the Schools for War "ABCs" was curriculum. "Public schools are geared to war," judged the *New York Times* in August 1943, and Indianapolis could proudly boast that its public schools had "adjusted their program of studies and their activities to the war." Although it could and would be interpreted as indoctrination and propaganda, this change in educational direction also offered the potential of positive attitudinal shift: a concept of "one world" in sharp contrast to Nazi racial hierarchal theories of superiority. In Chicago, for example, suggestions for Negro history or "Brown Studies" would be woven into general class material from first through eighth grade with stories of inspiration and histories of integration involving such figures as George Washington Carver, Marian Anderson, and Paul Robeson. Even one-room country schoolhouses strived for ideals of diversity during the Second World War. In memoirs from the Wyoming Retired Teachers' Association, schoolteacher Ruth Linder remembered the positive direction of wartime study among children and their parents who were now looking at maps and geography with a "keen" interest in world affairs.[33]

This school wartime curriculum, therefore, required a drastic reevaluation of what was taught as well as how and why. In the summer of 1942, five hundred New York City teachers participated in a workshop titled "War and the Curriculum" as they inquired about children's participation in the war effort. By the end of the first year of war, the New York City school system had prepared a report titled "All the Children" that advised that "courses of study now stress the principles underlying the fight of democracy against Nazism."[34]

Suggestions for New York City's schools included the use of composition to describe air warfare, history to emphasize democracy, and art to design war bond posters. National publications proudly proclaimed these particular changes: "Pupils write about planes, count air mileage, and spell torpedo." Other curriculum changes included the analysis of propaganda in English classes, the addition of military words such as "bombardier" and "fuselage" to spelling lists, a concentration on military themes in composition, the use of mathematical aviation problems for arithmetic, and development of new formulas to create synthetic rubber in chemistry. In wartime New York City, even nature study could now analyze "the ways zebras, grasshoppers and worms are camouflaged." Still, educators recognized that they must avoid any comparisons to the 1938 Nazi school curriculum directives that had enforced fascist ideological content even in such subjects as physics, arithmetic, and geography.[35]

These Nazi curriculum dangers were reflected in a 1942 Walt Disney animated film, *Education for Death*, based on the research of a best-selling study by Gregor Ziemer entitled *Hitler's Children* in which Ziemer described how Nazi ideology was imposed in German classrooms. *Time* described Disney's version as "a Nazified fairy tale" in which "the handsome armored prince (Hitler) wakes the rotund, snoozing princess (Germany)." *Newsweek* further characterized the plot: "Disney begins with Hitler as a comic-strip Siegfried awakening a sleeping, potbellied Germania to a New Order that specializes in snatching the young male from his cradle and 'heiling' him through Pimpf, Jungvolk, Hitler Jugen, and Storm Trooper to the white cross that marks his lebensbraum in a Nazi graveyard." This Nazi approach terrified most American teachers and parents, even startling a group of "tough" Manhattan kids who had previewed another more realistic film version of the Nazi school system. The students quickly concluded that "they were not so abused by their teachers as they had thought."[36]

Interestingly, Nazi-style education was also responsible for creating a more sophisticated and effective style of presentation in the classroom. The Third Reich had amassed an impressive centralized repository of eight thousand educational lantern slides and three hundred movies, and by the end of the war, educators in other European countries felt almost obligated to alter their classroom presentation styles and resources in "a grudging tribute to the effectiveness of Nazi teaching methods."[37]

In the United States, the war years not only promoted propaganda for Americanism but encouraged a new obligation toward war bonds and created a new war-based curriculum. The war years also intensified several issues that had challenged American school districts for decades: teacher shortages, overcrowded classes, drop-out rates, and child health issues.

"The teacher shortage threatens your child," announced *Parents* magazine in October 1943. The article suggested that the teacher shortage indicated "the first sign of educational collapse" as many qualified teachers could, in time of war, leave for better-paying defense jobs. The shortage had been detected before Pearl Harbor with an estimated deficit of 60,000 teachers in rural areas that appeared responsible for lower educational standards. By 1941 the Kansas Board of Education believed its only course was to lower teaching requirements because teachers were abandoning one-room schoolhouses "in droves."[38]

In 1943, more than 15,000 teacher vacancies existed nationally and schools had issued over 36,000 emergency teaching certificates. *Time* reported a shortage of 75,000 teachers with 2,000 rural schools failing to open, and at least 2 million children receiving "an education below the standards considered acceptable a year ago." Substandard education seemed imminent across the country. In less than two years of war, drastic shifts in educational statistics and finances indicated the situation had become "very dire," and *Newsweek* described U.S. educational standards as "plummeting."[39]

Lowered qualifications for teaching certification and increasingly overcrowded classrooms became typical means to provide children some semblance of an education or at least keep them off the streets during the war years. In New York City public schools, classes from elementary through high school often numbered more than thirty-five students. *Time* pulled no punches in describing the city's educational system: "New York City's school kids come from homes that speak 40 different languages. They live in some of the world's worst slums, have one of the world's highest juvenile delinquency rates. In Harlem and Brooklyn no man's lands, boys sometimes frighten their teachers by pulling knives in classrooms. At least 5,000 of the city's schoolboys are chronic truants."[40]

The teacher shortage demanded immediate solutions. Based on 1943 reports from information gathered at 1,389 schools, the federal government strongly recommended that schools retain quality teachers by increasing teachers' salaries and hiring married women. In the school year of 1941–1942, average annual salaries across the nation had varied from $517 to $2,618 while teachers often earned $650 in rural areas and $2,422 in urban areas. By 1944, the national average had only climbed 10 percent to $1,507. Rather than follow federal recommendations, many schools simply created oversized classes as a way to cope with the teacher shortage.[41]

The most successful way to overcome the teacher shortage and keep children in reasonably sized classrooms was to hire married women, which meant changing an old employment rule. Many newly married women had not wanted to be dismissed from their positions in the first place, but during the Depression it had become increasingly difficult for women to retain employment when men were out of work. During the war years, married women who had been dismissed from their teaching contracts would now be asked (if not begged) by administrators to return to the classroom. When Mertie Harrison Leavitt's PTA president asked her to come back to the Bedford School during the war years because it could not open without her as a teacher, Leavitt could not have been happier. "Once again I was back where I really belonged," Levitt proudly recalled, "for I had developed a love for teaching."[42]

Frank Kraus, the principal and superintendent of Cody School District No. 6 in Wyoming, remembered far more difficult details of the teacher shortage. "The most frustrating problem that was ever present during the war," Kraus recalled, "was keeping a competent staff of teachers in the school." He continued, "Almost every month one or more teachers were called to the service; others took positions in larger schools for higher wages or more desirable locations, and others went into other lines of work. I doubt if the schools in District No. 6, or any other district for that matter, could have kept their schools open without the help of these people [married women]." Superintendent Kraus concluded with high praise for the teachers who taught not only for love but for country: "They were truly the unsung heroines of WWII on the home front."

Whether through the force of renewed Americanism, the constant prompting for war bond contributions, or in the guise of wartime curriculum changes, the war had entered the schools, and the lure of better-paid defense jobs tempted not only teachers away from their classrooms but teenagers as well. Because of this fear that students would "abandon their studies for war jobs," Superintendent John Wade reemphasized his public plea to New York City in the autumn of 1943: "I will also reiterate my statement of last week when I expressed the hope that school-age children stay in school."[43]

Teenagers leaving high school became a constant problem during the war years. As early as 1942, the Department of Education created a radio series called "Children in Wartime" in an attempt to counteract this trend. The dramatic announcer need not have exaggerated the soon-to-be chronic high school dropout rate, but he did: "To Serve Your Country, Go to School. The war in which the United States is engaged today is a war to defend our democratic way of life, and the right of our children to live that way!" Teenage enrollment declined from 6,142,000 in 1942 to 5,761,000 in 1943; by 1944 thirty-two states were compelled to adopt an official "Go-to-School" program.[44]

During the Second World War, teenagers could easily obtain defense jobs with higher wages, but many adults remembered when the lucrative employment market during the Great War had proven temporary. This new Go-to-School drive aimed to capture Americans' already scattered attention with the classic democratic ideal that "an education is the rightful heritage of every child." Educators began to push for more creative rather than compulsory education laws, and the War Department, the Navy Department, and even the War Manpower Commission endorsed and implemented the message, through the Office of War Information, that "all children go to school even in wartime."[45]

In the first three decades of the twentieth century, children had spent increasingly more time in school than on the job, but now the lure of wartime employment and its paycheck reversed that modern trend of education. As Bing Crosby lilted in a movie short designed to keep teenagers in school, "And by the way, if you hate to go to school, you may grow up to be a mule." Other film clips contained less corny back-to-school pleas from Frank Sinatra, the Lone Ranger, and the Quiz Kids. In three years, the nation had lost 1 million high school students to wartime jobs. Seventeen-year-old Delores Sujah from Chicago exemplified the trend: "I didn't like school very much. This is essential work, and besides, there's a future."[46]

The dropout problem was not confined to urban areas. Rural schools had long endorsed "corn husking vacations," but when it was proposed to keep high school boys in the farm fields for half the school year, an alarming 34 percent of the men in Iowa farm families and 28 percent of the women approved of the idea. *Wallaces Farmer* countered its poll with an editorial statement: "But, so far, a majority of Iowa farm people want the big boys to stay in school and take the regular high school course, even tho the farm is short-handed and the old folks have to work extra hours."[47]

Attendance and resources were an ongoing problem for rural areas. More than 2.5 million American children still attended one-room schoolhouses in the countryside while 12.1 million attended only slightly larger rural schoolhouses, and at the first White House Conference on Rural Education in 1939, President Roosevelt endorsed a federal aid program for rural schools as necessary to raise educational standards. Within a year after Pearl Harbor, two thousand rural schools had closed for lack of teachers. Dr. Katherine Lenroot, chief of the Children's Bureau, also deplored the high numbers of children employed in rural economies and the poor rates of school attendance. As Eleanor Roosevelt concluded at the conference, "All of us in our States know it is sometimes harder for children in the rural areas to get the same advantages as children in the city areas."[48]

War also served to awaken the nation about the consequences of few health resources for children during the Great Depression. Chronic health issues related to poverty haunted many of the nation's schoolchildren, and one proposed solution was to enlist the schools in nutrition education, especially through the establishment of hot-lunch programs. During the 1942–1943 school year the federal government initiated a policy to provide a half-pint of milk to all students at a cost of one cent per day. In Maine, an estimated half of the state's schoolchildren took advantage of the new program. More than 300,000 of New York City's children bought penny milk, and another 75,000 children relied on free milk distributed in the public and parochial schools. When the New York state legislature wanted to halt subsidies of one-cent milk in 1943, the distressed mayor pleaded that almost 400,000 children would be affected.

Schools could provide consistent nutrition in some students' hard-pressed lives. When a rural New York elementary teacher smelled an orange in her classroom one morning, she stopped her class: "Someone must have forgotten to finish breakfast this morning. Stand up, whoever hasn't had breakfast." As the reporter noted, "All but six of the forty children gravely got to their feet."[49] Was this America, a country determined to have the best-fed army in the world, when so many of its own children did not enjoy ample or even adequate nutrition even in their public schools?

Another lesson carried from the Great Depression through the war years was the nutritional importance of regular hot lunches for many underprivileged children. As the usually nostalgic *Saturday Evening Post* described, the impact of the coordinated federal hot-lunch program should be direct and dramatic: "The Kids Aren't Hungry Any More." More than 93,000 schools across the country with 6.2 million children had joined hot-lunch programs by the beginning of World War II, and as the patriotic push promised, "They got it, like their teaching, without regard to race, color, creed, or means." In one Indiana school, 113 children gained half a ton in weight in one semester, and in a Minnesota school with an expanded hot-lunch program, the "student policeman" no longer patrolled the lunchroom because, as one young volunteer neatly explained to his principal, "More food, no fights."[50]

The nation should not forget the need for hot lunches for schoolchildren, *Wallaces Farmer* declared. "Farmers the country over are producing food for freedom, food for our armed forces, food for our factory workers, food for our fighting allies, food vital for victory, food to win the war and write the peace, food in ever-increasing amounts to feed the hungry of the devastated and ravaged lands as they are liberated."[51]

Maine's Representative Margaret Chase Smith had consistently promoted the nutritional value of hot lunches at public schools and noted how many children in her state had suffered bone defects from lack of vitamin D along with bad teeth and poor physical development from lack of vitamin C. Representative Smith believed that "some form of public support for school lunches has proven one of the cheapest and most effective ways of equalizing nutritional opportunity for children at an age when it is so critical that they have them if they are to have well-formed, vigorous bodies." Marion Sweetman, chairman of the Maine State Nutrition Committee, agreed: "A school lunch offers a short-cut to improved nutrition because the common deficiencies of the home diet can be remedied without the necessity of reaching and convincing each parent." Still, debate over the nutrition bill continued with some congressional members perceiving these funds as "federal intervention" and others as "part of the tendency to equalize educational opportunity." "This bill is in the Senate Committee on Agriculture," Smith sadly concluded in the spring of 1945, "and I am unable to find any move toward action on it."[52]

Teachers, ever mindful of their students' immediate needs, often took simple and direct action despite muddled and time-consuming political fights. One Cincinnati teacher took it upon herself to send a personal note addressed to a troubled wartime parent. "Even if you can't afford the five cents for the milk," the teacher wrote, "will you please sign the notice? I'd like Mary to have the milk, and I'll be glad to pay for it."[53]

World War II presented children with complex events and issues, altering the physical and emotional patterns of their daily lives in school. They had to fulfill multiple roles imposed by the drama of the outside world's chaos instead of the peaceful routines that young children crave, yet they persevered in their duties and more than accomplished the motto of Schools for War: Save, Serve, Conserve.

■ ■ ■

On "Victory in Europe Day" (May 8, 1945), Robert Schreiber, an elementary student from Rockford, Illinois, spent an exhilarating day with his shortwave radio after he had strung a long wire out his bedroom window and tied it to a tree for better reception. Robert kept running downstairs with updates for his mother who worried deeply about her brother in the armed forces. Even the news of V-E Day did not seem to calm her, though when Robert's father returned home later that day he uttered, "Thank God." The war may have ended in Europe, but on the home front children carried on. "My last clear memory," Robert recounted, "is of huddling next to the radio late into the night to hear more news of which there was precious little. And then I did my homework for the next day."[54]

3
Kid Salvage

"Victory Gardens Help"

Grow vim, vigor, and vitamins
Arm the Nation with food and health
Relieve transportation burdens
Decorate the home and landscape
Educate in morale and self-sufficiency
Nail the lie that United States youth is soft
Supply canned goods for soldiers.

—*Education for Victory* (July 1942)

"How many bullets will this make, mister?" the little boy inquired as he handed over his beloved toy train set. The advertisement embellished already emotional scrap drives with its sentimental copy: "Sacrifice isn't a thing you can weigh in pounds or count in dollars. It is measured in the brave little gifts of children."[1] And every child was expected to sacrifice in the nation's all-out campaigns for scrap material—tiny babies were to give up rubber pants, little girls were to give up rubber dolls, and young boys with polio were to give up old rubber tips from crutches. Every child could and should participate while also encouraging, even demanding, that adults do their share too. Why? Because the United States desperately needed the raw materials to conduct an industrial war.

The scrap drive contributions made by children—the "scrappers" who composed a 30-million-member army—became a story of individual initiative, cooperative ingenuity, and team creativity, but beneath the nostalgic story of little heroes sacrificing on the home front remained some serious concerns about adults' demands of time, strength, and endurance on particularly young children. A legacy of hard work endures for the generation who grew up during the Second World War, but the guilt lingers on as well: Am I working hard enough?

Early in the war, the *Atlanta Constitution*, expressive of many adult versions of scrap drive efforts, described the nation's youth as "anxious to serve." "It is a truism of the times," the Atlanta editorial began, "that total war demands participation of every American citizen." The newspaper praised "the cooperation of young people" but also compared America's children to the Nazis': "The youth of Germany helped Hitler rise to power. Now the youth of America have an opportunity to help this country and our allies crush that power, that force which has set the globe in flames."[2]

At first the scrap efforts were creative yet piecemeal events. But as the war progressed, many more coordinated events, focused campaigns, enthusiastic competitions, and innovative drives were conducted on national and local levels to collect not only raw resources for war munitions but also to grow fruits and vegetables as part of the Food for Freedom campaign. Even for children, military terms and motivations characterized these projects, such as the 1941 Armistice Day "War against Waste" in which teenage girls from the New York City Children's Aid Society sewed discarded apparel and flour sacks into useful clothing.[3] Early in the war, these campaigns emphasized reclaiming efforts, but as the war intensified, most of the effort shifted to recycling raw materials for industrial warfare.

The historian Bruce Smith, author of *The War Comes to Plum Street*, offers in his memoir the traditional viewpoint of the scrap drive efforts: "The Boy Scouts, 4-H clubs, community groups, and service stations all participated in this effort as housewives gave up their aluminum pots and pans, kids searched garages and trash areas for old tires and inner tubes, and everything from bedsprings to sewing machines to engine blocks accumulated at designated collection points." Often "a carrot" would be dangled in front of the children who participated in these community drives such as for an "enterprising group" of Indiana kids, who received free movie tickets for their 930 pounds of collected rubber items.[4]

Now that the scrap drives have taken on a sentimental, patriotic, almost heroic cast, it is easy to forget that these sometimes fun and often creative efforts went toward the very real and even desperate need to make bullets, bombs, tanks, jeeps, ships, and airplanes. Looking back, the campaigns appear quaint yet necessary. Although the cooperative efforts certainly elevated wartime morale, historians now question whether this scrap material was ever effectively used for the war effort; at the time there seemed to be little doubt. As Herbert Agar wrote in *Parents* magazine in 1942, "The way to win the war was for everyone to feel some responsibility. Even the

A girl in an aluminum drive. Courtesy of the University of Hawaii Archives.

youngest child can have the feeling that he has an important part to play." But the tactics used to promote enthusiasm for scrap drives might now be viewed uncomfortably when, for example, the Lincoln High School students from Portland posed for a publicity shot next to the banner, "Let's Help Slap the Jap Right Off the Map with Our Scrap."[5]

The historian Robert William Kirk best captures the complex relationship built up around children's scrap efforts in *Earning Their Stripes*. "The degree to which children's efforts in wartime scrap drives contributed to Allied victory cannot be known with certainty," Kirk acknowledges. "What is certain is that they saved countless hours of labor that adults would have had to devote to collecting rubber, metals, and salvage paper. They contributed to the positive impression, for the benefit of GIs and allies, that the nation was waging total war. In this regard, children served as good examples for adults. Nobody doubted that children's contribution was immense." As one example, an eleven-year-old boy named Jimmy Hargis from the Boise Sight Saving School in North Portland won the "Scrap for Victory" drive by single-handedly collecting more than four thousand pounds of reusable materials with his little red wagon. He won a $150 war bond for his effort and pledged to do more. "I gotta help win the war some way," Jimmy explained. "And I'm goin' to keep right on collectin' and mowin' lawns for defense stamps till she's over too."[6] Yet the question remains: Were the scrap drives patriotic and cheerful volunteerism or coercive and exploitative?

Children, already organized into groups such as the Boy Scouts, Girl Scouts, Boys' Clubs, Camp Fire Girls, Future Farmers of America (FFA), and 4-H clubs, actively participated in a variety of nationally organized but locally driven scrap campaigns. Informal neighborhood groups developed too as encouraged by media slogans. *Jack and Jill* magazine published a six-part series called "The Scrappers' Club," and even Little Orphan Annie promoted a cartoon gang called "The Junior Commandos," which was later transformed into actual neighborhood units. As the *New York Times* described all children's participation, "They are ready for the scrap."[7]

The Boy Scouts became the most militantly organized and motivated of the children's organizations, remaining throughout the war the most visible and consistent of "the scrappers." When General M'Donnell spoke to two hundred business leaders at the Reveille Breakfast in 1942, the Air Force officer stressed the important role that the New York Boy Scouts would play in the Civilian Defense Plan. As the general declared, "The training of a Boy Scout makes him a better soldier and a better American because it builds discipline and patriotism." Or as a Ralston ad announced under an illustration of hard-working Boy Scouts, "We've got a job to do!" A *Saturday Evening Post* cartoon portrayed a Boy Scout with his pet goat nicknamed "my salvage detector." Other published illustrations, such as a cartoon in *Time*, portrayed "Boy Scouts at War." The cartoon caption recalled the days when Scouts simply took nature hikes but had now become "Public Scavenger Service No. 1."[8]

Examples of Scout efforts, both individual and collective, could be dramatic, such as that of thirteen-year-old "Star Scout" Daniel Flory of Lancaster, Pennsylvania, who "marched up and down the streets politely ringing doorbells, politely asking housewives for old newspapers." In seven afternoons little Daniel, himself weighing only 84 pounds, collected over 9,500 pounds of paper, rather large loads for his little wagon. Nationally in this campaign, Boy Scouts collected 300 million pounds of wastepaper. "The hard-working Scouts are wooed by every Government agency," *Time* reported. "Reason: everything the 1,500,000 Boy Scouts and Cubs undertake reaches astronomical statistics of success. They hung up 1,607,500 defense bonds and stamp posters throughout the country, collected 10,500,000 of the 12,000,000 lbs of aluminum contributed in all the nation, on Baseball Defense Bond Day 3,722 Scouts delivered 260,939 pieces of Treasury Department literature in 121 baseball stadiums." Although the *Time* report expressed some concern that perhaps the Boy Scouts worked too hard as children, advertisers never hesitated to capitalize on the children's scrap-driving images such as Royal Crown Cola's Boy Scout Britt who was "rounding up scrap all day," Westinghouse's image of two Boy Scouts collecting tin cans, or Campbell Soup's "wartime meals" for children collecting scrap.[9]

The Girl Scouts' adult leaders also applauded their young scouts' roles in the war effort. Virginia Lewis, consulting psychologist for the British National Girl Reserves, believed some duties for young girls during wartime brought "cause for concern," such as late-night air raid duties or the entertaining of servicemen; Lewis thought child care, farm work, gardening, knitting, sewing, and salvage duties more appropriate girls' responsibilities within a civilian defense program. Leaders of the Girl Scouts also attributed the success of their scouts to their training. As Mrs. Winthrop Aldrich, chairman of the Greater New York Civilian Defense Organization, observed, "I think it is fair to say that this is largely due to the training in patriotism and usefulness that the Girl Scouts have received in recent years." Mrs. Theodore Roosevelt Jr., the reelected president of the Council, declared the country to be "doubly strong" with its significant numbers of female participants. "There have always been heroines," Mrs. Roosevelt remarked, "but now we march with men and serve in whatever way we are found to be most effective." The Girl Scout Home Front Reserve numbered more than half a million, with Girl Scouts determined to be "as busy as the factory workers and just as conscious of their place in the war effort."[10]

"Junk makes fighting weapons," declared *Successful Farming* in an advertisement for the War Production Board's list of needed materials, especially scrap iron and old rubber. Future Farmers of America—groups for high school boys enrolled in agricultural programs—also proved to be exceptional workers in the scrap iron drives with ready access to farm supplies and transportation. Iowa's FFA chapters noted in their *Special Report of Wartime Activities* that these young farmers had collected 665,975 pounds of scrap metal, 171,750 pounds of paper, and 61,202 pounds of rubber in one year's time. As the small-town FFA instructor for Winterset, Iowa, Simon Ossian described the boys' salvage work in exacting military terms. "They worked like troopers," Ossian recalled, "never giving up until they had combed ditches, junk piles, and other remote places to find scrap metal and rubber." This local FFA troop collected 20.8 tons of metal and 400 pounds of rubber, netting $155.12 to buy war bonds for their local organization. The Winterset High School yearbook called this scrap drive "one big achievement."[11]

International Harvester thanked both rural adults and children for the tons of scrap collected in their "harvest of the metal crop" when ten thousand farming communities collected more than a million and a half tons. In Moravia, Iowa, thirty-two FFA members collected a hundred tons of scrap and persuaded local farmers to find an additional two hundred tons.[12]

In the 4-H "Call to Service," rural girls became a strong part of the organization's 1.5-million-member "army" when even occasional bugle calls summoned 4-H girls to duty. "As a farm girl, you will do your part in the food production program," the 4-H promotional pamphlet began. "You will work to conserve clothing and equipment and will save useful scrap materials for war uses." 4-Hers collected tons of scrap material in 1943, according to *Successful Farming*, and the numbers continued to be impressive. 4-H had always prided itself on its recordkeeping and work ethic, and their wartime numbers remain significant contributions: its achievements "boosted America's food arsenal in 1943 by 5,000,000 bushels of Victory Garden products; 90,000 head of dairy cattle; 600,000 head of livestock; 9,000,000 fowl; and 12,000,000 pounds of legumes; and contributed to the direct war effort by 12,000,000 pounds of scrap and $14,000,000 worth of War Bonds and Stamps." This record of production and leadership culminated nationally with an estimated 50,000 4-H girls who canned more than 20 million quarts of food as well as collecting tons of scrap material and pursuing other recycling efforts. The 4-H clubs proclaimed, "It's the story of youth trying to make the best better."[13]

Boys' Club members also joined in the scrap efforts with individual efforts and publicized propaganda events. An eleven-year-old from Chicago received the first official Victory Volunteers badge from Paul McNutt, director of the Federal Security Administration, for his efforts in a local scrap drive. As a longtime Boys' Club supporter, former president Herbert Hoover also lauded the young Victory Volunteers scrap collections and their "thousand duties," from making fire alarm boxes to working as hospital orderlies. "The boys are gathering up an unbelievable amount," Hoover boasted, "of scrap iron, brass, tin, paper, and whatnot. They use the money from this scrap for their club purpose and donations to the nation's armed forces."[15]

On their thirty-first anniversary, the Camp Fire Girls mobilized the Thriftee Army with a concentration on conservation. "The Thriftee Army is a battle against waste," as the *Los Angeles Times* pitched it, "and they're fighting it on three fronts: every penny for war bonds, rooting out waste materials, and reinforcing home and personal equipment so any extra money can go to war bonds."[16]

Amid these accomplishments, a few cautious voices emerged, especially during the early years of home-front activity. Child development experts, such as the author of a *Parents* article titled "Childhood as Usual?" acknowledged that boys and girls collected scrap enthusiastically, but they asked the pertinent question, "How much should a child participate in the war effort?" As the noted child psychologist Anna W. M. Wolf commented in "War and Discipline," "With military discipline the order of the day, must we now revise our modern ideas of discipline by guidance rather than coercion?"[14]

During the war years, both boys' and girls' organizations established highly militaristic styles, standards, and methods. The children, with their adult leaders, formed battalions, waged war, earned medals, and blasted enemies, all in an effort to raise the necessary materials to conduct war. Clubs formed armies, recreation turned to the search for salvage, citizens became soldiers. Young students at Hunter College Elementary School in New York City decided to stage "a salvage masquerade." These four hundred children sang patriotic songs while dressed in tin-can sombreros and nylon stocking hula skirts. An eight-year-old student named Michael Sahl played the piano for the pageant and sang a solo of his own creative composition, "Scrap Soldier": "We'll go from house to house collecting scrap for salvage. Calling fathers, calling mothers, calling sisters, calling brothers: Be a scrap soldier today."[17]

John Adams Junior High School in Santa Monica, California, concentrated on the actual gathering rather than singing about scrap metal, and these students collected more than 26 tons of material—farm equipment, knickknacks, train wheels, water tanks, and even several automobiles. One teacher noted the students' not quite patriotic—but perhaps age-appropriate—response: "They're happy because the building was so cluttered up that classes had to be cancelled. Junk was piled so high in corridors and entrances that students couldn't get to their desks." In another California city, 300,000 Los Angeles schoolchildren held a two-week scrap drive to collect metal, rubber, and rags. "So Uncle Sam's war production plants will have sufficient material," the promoters promised, "to make the ships, tanks, and guns for the youngsters' big brothers on the battle fronts." Belvedier Junior High School collected 3,000 pounds of salvage.[18]

Humorous illustrations noted children's diligence, if not their overenthusiasm, in rounding up scrap metal such as the little boys in a *Saturday Evening Post* cartoon titled "Scrap the Axis!" in which the boys meow like alley cats so that metal goods will be thrown out the windows for easy collecting. Or the Emerson Electric advertisement in which two boys enthusiastically collect junk until an adult reminds them to be careful with their process: "Here . . . Here . . . that fan isn't scrap!" Or the cartoon in which a boy receives a bronze medal for scrap metal resourcefulness along with the admonishment, "Now, young man, what are you going to do with this bronze medal?"[19]

Another scrap item needed throughout the duration of the war was paper, and urban children had the greatest access to this material. In 1942 New York's children, ages six to twelve, individually lugged twenty-pound bundles of waste paper into the Jones Center of the Children's Aid Society, receiving ten cents a load for defense stamps. Some children even "rigged up" a sales booth with a "Punch and Judy" stage. When New York conducted its city scrap drive in the summer of 1944, the five children who collected the most salvaged material were honored as luncheon guests at the Hotel Bristol. Despite unending heat, children had collected citywide 67.7 tons of paper via 305 playgrounds, and the week's winner was the summer playground team of Public School #179. For their press photograph, the proud little boys waved their scrap drive prizes—tickets to Steeplechase Park.[20]

The Summer Playground team of P.S. 179, winners in the citywide playground drive for waste paper salvage. Courtesy of the New York State Archives.

Later that fall, the War Production Board established the Paper Trooper Program, which made "school children officially members of our war production machinery." Although *Education for Victory* had published a tentative article asking why the nation depended so heavily on children's work to collect wastepaper, later propaganda certainly overrode such concerns with posters boldly proclaiming "Save a Bundle a Week—Save Some Boy's Life."[21]

The Paper Trooper Program proceeded without opposition and developed a WPB shoulder insignia along with a P-T arm patch for each participating child who collected a hundred pounds of paper. The Paper Trooper manual reminded children of annual numerical goals: the United States needed 8 million tons of wastepaper in seven-pound bundles. By war's end, Paper Trooper stories and posters ranged from sadly poignant to outrageously propagandistic. In one tale titled "The Champ," eight-year-old Billy Hamilton of Brooklyn emerged as the champion paper collector in his neighborhood despite "getting around on crutches." Or as a nationally distributed poster proclaimed in the harsh phrasing of the day, "These Paper Troopers won't stop collecting waste paper till the last Jap surrenders."[22]

Even before the attack on Pearl Harbor, the drive to collect aluminum had begun in July 1941, coordinated by the Civilian Defense Office. Called Tea Kettles for Airships, it offered a publicity photograph in the Kiwanis Magazine of three congressional women with a notation that "the women were giving up part of their kitchen equipment to be made into bigger and better bombers." The Boy Scouts as the actual collection agents stood in the background on a heavily loaded truck. In Los Angeles and other cities across the country, children walked door-to-door collecting aluminum cooking pots. One slogan simply stated, "Aluminate Hitler."[23]

Although authorities encouraged children to be aggressive in these various scrap drives, most of the promotional literature suggested that the children responded because of "a need to be needed." A 1942 survey of the Boy Scouts revealed that they had collected 10.5 million pounds of the 12 million pounds of aluminum collected nationally, a phenomenal achievement. "We've been told that children, like the rest of us," the Boy Scout spokesperson said, "need to feel that we are all in this fight together and they are holding up their end."[24]

Taking a humorous look at the children's scrap search, the *Saturday Evening Post* published cartoons about the aluminum and tin drives. In one, two children walk to school, carrying their band instruments as one young musician declares, "It certainly is a shame they didn't make these things out of aluminum!" In another cartoon, a little boy suggests to a little girl, "May I carry your tin cans to school tomorrow?"[25]

Some promotional activities, however, were not so cute. "This is what the Japs did to Susan Julia, aged ten months," began a *Life* article. When the baby girl's last pair of latex pants had torn, her father repaired them with a tube patch from the auto store. Never one to resist a good pun, the *Life* reporter quipped, "Now Susan is getting lots more mileage out of her old pants."[26]

To hold adults' interest, the various scrap drives had to be packaged and repackaged with various emotional approaches, but the younger generation seemed to be more easily motivated. Nine-year-old Ray Haber of Des Moines—a flag in one hand and a toy six-shooter in his holster—appeared to be "spurred on" by the reward of a penny a pound for scrap rubber. But the emotional tugs could also be severe. "Her dad is Jap prisoner," stated one newspaper headline. "Scrap rubber contributions will help win the war, and when the war is over, Arlene Hellyer, eight, will see her dad again."[27]

The rubber emergency affected all ages and items from baby pants to adults' automobile tires, from little girls' treasured dolls to dogs' ragged toy bones (even those of President Roosevelt's little dog Fala). A young boy with polio even donated the rubber tips from his crutches. No personal sacrifice was too small or too great.[28]

A memorable and unusual scrap collection, one involving no sacrifice whatsoever but rather good outdoor fun for children, was the milkweed drive. In the late summer of 1944, the War Food Administration announced that it needed 1.5 million pounds of milkweed floss to replace kapok in military life jackets and called for "an army of milkweed pod harvesters." Boy Scouts, Girl Scouts, Camp Fire Girls, 4-H clubs, the Junior Red Cross, and other youth organizations signed up for various competitive milkweed drives, but one-room country schoolhouses provided the most ready army of collectors, closest to the natural source. Armed with mesh harvest bags, these enthusiastic rural children escaped from classrooms to search for the light green prickly pods—motivated by not only military necessity but perhaps a legitimate leave from homework and twenty cents per bushel-sized bag. The champion of Iowa's Statewide Rural School Milkweed Pod Contest was LeRoy Powers, age ten, from Emmetsburg, who collected 150 bushels for "use in war production." In Kossuth County, Iowa, schoolchildren collected enough pods to fill half a train car and received $450 as a donation to their school. Ellen Witham was the county's individual "bag champ," as she collected 44 of her rural school's 58 bags. Iowa's children collectively gathered 100,000 to 150,000 bushel bags, but Michigan led the national drive with 700,000 bags of milkweed pods.[29]

While salvaging was defined as the recycling of resources for the war effort, rationing was meant to conserve other resources. "Sacrifice" became the key word, but most Americans certainly realized that their own shortages never approached the hardships of the Allies in Great Britain or Russia. When Britain's Lord Woolton, Minister of Food, announced a strict rationing system in 1940, these restrictions continued long after the war until 1954. American citizens, on the other hand, always viewed rationing as a short-term solution to a wartime problem. Rationing was imposed on the following commodities: automobiles, February 1942; sugar, May 4, 1942; fuel oil, October 12, 1942; coffee, November 21, 1942; gasoline, December 1, 1942; processed/canned food, February 2, 1943; shoes, February 7, 1943; and meats and fats, March 29, 1943.[30]

The distribution of ration books, as described by the historian Mary Martha Thomas, became "the biggest job ever undertaken by our government—the issuance of a food ration book for every citizen." In his book *Let the Good Times Roll*, historian Paul Casdorph portrays rationing in 1943 as extremely difficult, when "approximately thirty-five-million housewives trudged to thousands of schoolhouses in late February to get the books." But most Americans made the best of the circumstances, and undoubtedly women staunchly faced the food rationing system and displayed their ingenuity with alternative recipes. "I worried about birthday cakes," recalled Robert Monroe Keenan. As her twelfth birthday approached, Roberta's mother found a recipe for a Karo-syrup cake. "The cake was so sticky it stuck to your fingers when you touched it," Roberta remembered. "There was no tidy way to eat it, but we didn't care—it was sweet and festive."[31]

Every American home faced the challenge of balancing needs with wants—sometimes frustrating but ideally democratic. Since these shortages remained largely part of the kitchen front, most rationing was considered "women's work." The historians Karen Anderson and Doris Weatherford each found that women managed a disproportionate share of the burden of coping with civilian deprivation but also deserved credit for its success. Women who best coped with rationing lived in small towns and on farms where they had "land and supplies—and foresight—to garden and preserve their own supply." Young families faced the most difficult straits of time, money, and community resources. As Weatherford comments in a sad irony, "The people who were most badly provided for by rationing were the wives and young children of soldiers asked to lay down their lives."[32]

At rare times, children proved to be a severe challenge to the conservation scheme. One little girl actually ate her mother's ration book, and many other children probably "helped" their parents misplace the valuable booklets. In a *Saturday Evening Post* cartoon, a mother reads a war-era bedtime story to her little girl. "And in the end," she concludes, "they found their ration books, and lived happily ever after."[33]

Although Louisa Cook, an elementary school student from Michigan, knew her mother had been "watchful" of their family sugar supply, she wanted to surprise her mother with a birthday cake. Louisa, however, forgot to add the baking soda to the cake batter. Her brothers ate the first flat chocolate cake to hide the evidence as Louisa baked a second, but her little brothers could not keep the secret as one little boy proved to be "a blabbermouth." "Mother was happy with the birthday cake," Louisa remembered, "but she let me know that she had no appreciation for the amount of sugar I had used."[34]

With the proliferation of stories about starving children and the scarcity of food elsewhere in the world, American children became the target for a harsh lesson in charity. The image of foreign children's destitution would be effectively used for fund-raising. The United Nations War Relief was only one example of a particularly effective charity. The "story of one cent" became the United Nations' fund-raising mantra. One cent would purchase a meal in China, where 2 million children were suddenly orphans. One cent would also buy a meal in Greece, where thousands of children were dying each day from lack of milk and medicine. One cent could begin to provide "the barest necessities" to at least a million orphaned Russian children whose parents and relatives had lost their lives.[35] The Allies needed not only American munitions and military men but its help in feeding people, as food had become a serious weapon of war.

Since children had so often been encouraged not to waste their food and sometimes were punished if they did, the "clean plate," which had become a constant refrain during the Great Depression, earned a new formality during World War II. When a national "Clean Plate Club" began in Glencoe, Illinois, through the initiative of five-year-old Margot Chinnock and her seven-year-old brother John, children across the country could now formally take the pledge to "finish all the food on my plate and drink all of my milk, unless excused . . . until Uncle Sam has licked the Japs and Hitler." Otherwise, the consequence loomed as a child would have to turn in the coveted Clean Plate button. The cited penalty did fall to Betsy Brown, age five, who had refused to drink her milk, but when she finished the glass later, Betsy again became, according to the *Time* article, "a member in good standing." The *Minneapolis Tribune* (in a full-page ad in the *New York Times*) urged all American children to "clean their plates" and "Join America's Most Unexclusive Club."[36]

All children could contribute to the conservation of food, whether it was two-year-old Mickey having to snap his stick of candy in half to make it last longer or first graders Tommy and Barbara learning in school how to conserve rationed sugar by baking "war muffins." Like adults, American children never fully embraced rationing, but the democratic need for a systematic rationing mechanism was never questioned. Rationing distributed available food and relieved possible inflation. And sometimes it appealed to children's tastes: the blue box of Kraft Macaroni and Cheese Dinner became quite popular during the war years, substituting for rationed meat and dairy products as it only required only one ration coupon for its dried noodles and powdered cheese. In 1943, American families purchased 80 million of the blue boxes.[37]

What produced a great deal of enthusiasm—a practical morale booster and stress reliever as well—was the creation of victory gardens. Even Walt Disney's never-patient Donald Duck planted a victory garden, although Donald remained convinced that sabotage lurked around every garden corner. For most gardeners, however, nurturing their seeds gave them a sense of personal accomplishment as well as fulfilling a desperately needed wartime duty. As one little boy said to another in a *Saturday Evening Post* cartoon, "You just bury these seeds and pretty soon, bang, beans!"[38]

Honolulu stayed out in front with home gardens because of its tropical climate. Dedicated citizens formed five community gardens containing 8,000 individual plots and began cultivation by early March 1942, and forty local Boy Scouts from four troops also started garden projects across the islands. Later in the spring, more than 7,500 Boy Scouts in Los Angeles founded the Times Garden Club, "adding another to their list of good deeds."[39]

The incredible variety of victory garden locations ranged from the White House lawn to vacant lots in the Bronx. Diana, ten-year-old daughter of Harry Hopkins and a temporary resident at the White House, planted her victory garden of beans, carrots, tomatoes, and cabbage near President Roosevelt's study, hoping to have her vegetables served in the Executive Mansion. Other less fortunate but just as determined little girls labored in their victory gardens located in the Bronx backyard of the House of the Holy Comforter. These girls, suffering from chronic illnesses but believing in a hopeful future, surrounded themselves with growing "war plants."[40] At the Garden for Victory Achievement Day in Glenwood Springs, Colorado, in February 1942, "A Parsnip's Serenade" was sung for morale purposes to the melody "Tramp, Tramp, Tramp, the Boys Are Marching":

> When you're feeling down and out
> Don't care what it's all about
> And you've lost your pep and feeling mighty blue;
> Everything that you have tried
> Makes you feel all wrong inside,
> This is what will bring the sunshine
> Back to you.[41]

Victory gardening as directed and promoted through the public school systems yielded a coordinated program called School Gardening. Garden projects required some adult supervision during the summer months, and enthusiastic educators developed a Garden Project Score Card to rank their students' efforts and accomplishments. To earn a possible one hundred points, students had to appear interested and well informed about garden work generally as well as tend their plots. Along with the gardening, students received points for design, timeliness, activation, and thriftiness. Still, the School Gardening motto was scarcely pastoral: "Keeping up the fight!"[42]

Victory gardens crisscrossed the country. In a survey of Virginia schools, 23 of 71 county school divisions (almost one in three) reported a planned garden, but of thirteen city school divisions, only two had planted a city garden. Family numbers were more impressive: 17,688 of the country families and 414 city families served by the schools had increased their home garden production. School-directed gardening provided not only the instruction but also the organization and leadership required of community gardening for "substantial contributions." A backyard victory garden ideally measured two thousand square feet—no small enterprise. In Oklahoma, Native American families proved to be exceptional victory gardeners with a total of 36,200 gardens, or one to every two Native American families in the state. With an emphasis on healthy, necessary work, victory gardens became an official part of the Food for Freedom campaign. In a *Saturday Evening Post* cartoon, a little boy innocently appraised his recent victory garden efforts for his parents: "It seems strange that everything came up but the spinach!"[43]

The personal memories of these school-directed—or perhaps coerced—gardens seem to be mixed from a child's perspective. Charles Osgood remembers his father directing their family garden project in Baltimore. "Dad made us prepare a backyard plot," Osgood recalls, "about ten by fifteen feet, by digging the soil, removing the grass, weeds and stones, and raking the plot to plant the seeds for vegetables and flowers that we had gotten at school. It was the first manual labor of my life, labor that must have made me decide on a career in which I would be digging only for words." Osgood adds, "In addition to the terrible pumpkins, we planted lettuce, carrots, radishes, squash, marigolds, and daisies. How marigolds and daisies would be blows to the enemy I did not understand." Osgood also remembers receiving from his elementary teacher Sister Ursula the assignment to debate why victory gardens were "bad." As Osgood quips, this was, of course, the harder argument. "The following day at school," he recalls, "I made what may have been the first attack on victory gardens in American history."[44]

When 125 garden leaders gathered in Washington, D.C., in January 1944 for the National Victory Garden Conference, the extension director M. L. Wilson declared, "The Victory Garden movement of the second world war will go down in history as one of the greatest civilian activities ever stimulated and organized by man." Twenty million amateur gardeners had produced 40 percent of the fresh vegetable supply for 1943. Through gardening demonstrations, schools hoped to better teach such subjects as nature study, biology, nutrition, and home economics. When Betty Peek, age fifteen, of Geniss, North Carolina, became the national high school champion of the "Green Thumb Victory Garden Contest," she declared, "I learned more about a garden in one season than I probably would have learned in a lifetime had I not tried in the Victory Garden Contest." This farm girl's prize for cultivation of a fifty-by-hundred-foot garden was a $500 war bond.[45]

By the spring of 1945, a Victory Garden Medal, developed by the National Victory Garden Institute to honor General Douglas MacArthur, encouraged American boys and girls to continue gardening for the war effort. In a rare instance of understatement, General MacArthur himself answered the gardeners' call to duty: "Glad to do anything that will help."[46]

This image of the U.S. home front—especially its scrap drives and victory gardens—has remained relatively unscathed, the pride of dedicated citizens who remained productive and resourceful. Children were particularly adept in this collective effort—industrious, patient, creative, and focused when the world around them seemed anything but. Scrap drives and victory gardens became public displays of patriotic energy and devotion within which young children could excel.

Yet these public displays of patriotic commitment could also dramatize deep rifts and provoke anger in a wartime society. During the late spring of 1944 in Larchmont, New York, neighbors told a sad story about a Japanese American boy named Teddy Matsumota whose victory garden was vandalized. Teddy and his family had recently relocated to New York as displaced Japanese Americans from one of the ten Western internment camps. "We're sorry about your garden, Teddy," the local newspaper apologized. "You worked hard on it, and the beans and cabbages and tomatoes and strawberries were just beginning to flourish. The rows were neatly laid out, and there weren't any weeds. You and your mother have worked hard on it all through the spring. And then someone sneaked at night and ripped it all to pieces."

Larchmont's editor tried to explain the senseless act. "It has happened down through the generations to those who have tried to plant love and understanding and tolerance in the world," the editor wrote. "Just when the plants begin to grow, someone who doesn't understand tramps in and ruins the garden. But they have kept on planting and each time more of the seeds survive." Concerned citizens in the community decided to set a positive example when they replanted the Matsumota garden with their own seedlings.[47]

Victory gardens have always represented much more than just raising vegetables, and the postwar world would desperately need the sharing of food as well as other caring acts. Kindness between all citizens needed to be cultivated and salvaged for the possibility of a peaceful future world.

4

Junior Commandos

Be thankful American boys and girls can still play.

—Flexible Flyer advertisement, *Life* (December 8, 1942)

Life can never be all sombre where children are concerned.

—Sally Alderson, *War All Over the World: Childhood Memories of WWII from Twenty-three Countries* (2003)

On the Saturday morning following Pearl Harbor, an Iowa housewife took her egg money to Toyland to purchase two Tom Thumb tanks. "I'll probably step on one of these in the night and break a leg," she told the clerk. "But it'll at least keep us reminded that we're in war!" War toys had not been selling very quickly in Des Moines or even in Los Angeles until the attack of the Axis that week in December 1941. Now euphemistically called "defense toys," ideas abounded in what the *Los Angeles Times* titled this "Grim Yuletide": antiaircraft guns; two-person sidewalk tanks; model airplanes such as Thunderbolts, Hell Divers, and Tomahawks; miniature trains with attached camouflage cars; toy soldiers with battle dress and the latest weapons; board games called Build Your Own Defense, Axe the Axis, and Bombers Aloft; and even dolls with little sailor or nurse uniforms. As the *Times* concluded, "War is here—as far as toys are concerned."[1]

Even recently bombed Hawaii retained its optimism for this Christmas season and the wartime holidays to come. "Your old Uncle Santa Claus isn't downhearted—not a bit!" a Honolulu newspaper editor promised. "And he'll zoom in from the sky Christmas Eve, with his rarin' reindeer Dancer and Prancer pulling a big sleigh load of gifts for Hawaii folks. In

A boy in a cardboard tank. Courtesy of the State Historical Society of Iowa Archives.

other words, Christmas is coming right along, and not all the axis powers and their puppets in the wide, wide world are going to prevent it."[2]

But buying toys during a global war could seem frivolous or unpatriotic. The Treasury Department urged parents that holiday season and through 1945 to purchase "more significant gifts" than "trinkets and baubles and toys." The Treasury Department recommended giving "a defense bond, something that expresses the spirit of the season and at the same time helps the nation arm." One can quickly imagine the disappointed holiday looks, then and now, as a young boy or girl opened a gift to discover a government document rather than a brand new set of toy soldiers or a gleaming model airplane. Still, the war-bond propaganda continued to target children's play. One advertisement showed the well-known Uncle Sam image angrily pointing at a little boy—"I Want You!" The boy in the ad nervously tried to reply, "Bu—but I like to PLAY!" Uncle Sam responded even more harshly, "And you'll find there's no play in all the world that's as much fun as helping to build the world of the future."[3]

The day after President Roosevelt had appeared before Congress to ask for a declaration of war, a sixth grader from Philadelphia wrote to the president of his own youthful intentions. "I heard you on the radio at lunch time," John Cameron began. "I hope we win this war. I hope we can work and play without being bombed and I hope we can sleep without being bombed, I love this country and hope it will always be free." John signed his letter simply "An American Patriot." This world of war desperately needed workers of any age, and American children would no doubt work diligently for their country's war effort; but as John stated, they also wanted to play . . . just a little. Yet even a children's page in *Successful Farming*—ironically titled "The Playhouse"—continually emphasized responsible work for its young rural readers. "I know that as loyal Americans," the children's columnist wrote, "you'll work just as hard in school as you worked at home during the summer."[4]

Although children's lives during the Second World War now comprised long hours of volunteer and paid labor, American children needed respite from their patriotic duties in fields and factories, neighborhoods and schools. Play, as the historian Pamela Riney-Kehrburg points out in *Childhood on the Farm*, has always been "relatively unregulated": "The opportunity to play in many ways represented what it was to be a child: to run, to laugh, to exercise the imagination, and to be free of adult cares and responsibilities."[5]

Children in the 1940s were not as regulated as they are today, remembers Charles Osgood who was nine years old in Baltimore that first full year of war. Children did not lead scheduled lives as do present-day "wee CEOs." "In 1942, the words 'free play' weren't shameful because that was, happily, all we did," Osgood reflects. "Every kid made it all up, using only our own resources, and we never had a 'play date.'"[6]

Despite the expectations for industriousness of parents, schools, and government, boys and girls did find ways to play during wartime, expressing their hopes and fears, coping with their confusion and pain, inspiring their curiosity and courage, as well as releasing their anger and energy. Despite the world's conflicts, children improvised playtime, often impromptu battles attacking make-believe Nazis or bombing imaginary Japanese. Although sales of commercial toys plummeted under various rationing rules, sales of militaristic items for both boys and girls escalated with the first wartime holiday season of 1941 and continued throughout the next three years, quickly tapering off in 1945. Toys managed to be manufactured and marketed to American children throughout the war despite the rationing of priority materials, especially iron and lead. Guns, toy soldiers, model airplanes, tanks, jeeps, ships, militaristic board games, thematic books, and replica uniforms comprised the most consistently popular war toys.

Among toy guns, one rifle could shoot cork bullets more than thirty-five feet with "a first-class wallop!" Daisy air rifles added two noisier models called the Commando and the Chattermatic, and *Popular Mechanics* developed its own design for the "Bow Bazooka," which fired "harmless explosive rockets." The instructions advised, "Patterned after the army's famous bazooka, this play gun will make it easy for backyard soldiers to neutralize enemy pillboxes." *Popular Mechanics* also published several blueprints for wooden toy guns, which provided the necessary acoustics while avoiding the use of rationed metal. "Harmless" and "fun" became the most commonly used words to describe these children's guns. Even Nestlé cocoa adopted a militaristic advertising theme with an illustration of two little boys going out for morning play complete with tin helmets and machine guns as their smiling mother waved them on, promising, "Start the Day the Happy Way!"[7]

Holding either his toy tommy gun or a wooden machine gun, the grandson of President Roosevelt liked to stand watch during the war years positioned between two White House guards. Even with a toy gun, this prominent little boy's war play had an eerie reality because of its setting. Once the little Roosevelt "menacingly promised protection" to passing pedestrians: "I'll knock them off, if anybody comes."[8]

With global tensions spiraling, adults did not seem surprised that most children also caught "war fever." Child-care experts supported and even encouraged this perceived need for children's war expression through aggressive play. In a July 1942 article for *Parents*, "When Play Goes Warlike," the magazine suggested that children can maintain their "emotional balance" by expressing their anxieties through war play. The aim of such play was to "meet and deal" with "fear, intolerance, reprisals, biases, timidity and aggression and to rehearse courage, clear thinking, independent judgments and fresh values." Child-care experts cautioned that such phrases as "shoot those Japs" or "bomb those Nazis" should be regarded by parents only as "the need to unbottle fear and tension." "The war may last for some time," the *Parents* author concluded. "This is our children's one childhood: we must do all that is possible to let them grow and stretch to the very limit of the opportunities under the changing circumstances."[9]

Some parents seemed less confident about the harmless nature of war play. Shortly after Pearl Harbor, a mother from Washington, D.C., wrote to the *Post* about her concerns. "My eleven-year-old son seems delighted at the war," she began. "His walls are full of maps; he gets the news eagerly. He and his friends talk constantly about going out and 'blasting Hitler.' 'Just my luck,' he says, 'to live where there's no fighting. Boy! Would I love to have an air raid.' I find it hard to believe he is really so bloodthirsty." The *Post* advised this agitated mother that her son merely craved action and danger—all normal emotions for the time. In other words, war play was not cause for great worry.[10]

Another parent in the nation's capital wrote a week later about her own neighborhood concerns. "The boys on our block play nothing but war these days," she complained. "Their belts fairly bristle with toy guns and makeshift warplanes are constantly zooming through the air. Isn't the world full enough of this sort of thing without the children having to play at it? How can we stop it?" This mother received similar advice: "Don't try to stop this kind of war play. Play is the language of children, their way of working out the matters that concern them deeply at the moment." The *Post* continued, "Boys have always played games that release their war-like feelings. A certain amount of such play is needed by most normal young males at any time. Their need is even greater today when war surges all about them. Girls too feel this need now. They have to play out their heightened feelings, just as many of us older people need to talk ours out." Military play, like making conversation or composing letters, could express war worries and release tension along with a touch of humor. As the little boy informed his father in a *Saturday Evening Post* cartoon, "I forgot to tell you, Pop—I mined the bathtub!"[11]

During the war, some older adults lamented the apparent loss of their cherished childhood games such as mumblety-peg, follow the leader, roly poly, and fox and hounds. Now children's playful energies seemed directed only toward warlike games, as Frank Sullivan colorfully described in a *Good Housekeeping* article. "Around my neighborhood these days, and no doubt around yours also," Sullivan began, "the welkin rings each afternoon after school with that ferocious, guttural, staccato noise indicating that a small boy, in the capacity of a Spitfire or Hurricane, is raking a squadron of Zeros or Stukas, represented by other small boys, with a withering machine-gun fire." Although Sullivan appeared nostalgic for his own lost boyhood games, he felt unconcerned about this new style of aggressive wartime play. His description of these make-believe soldiers was playful: "The carnage is awful. Each side is annihilated; but, happily, the warriors always deannihilate themselves in time to get home for supper," Sullivan concluded. "Eavesdropping on these martial pastimes one day, I found myself wondering if the youngsters of this age of Flash Gordon and Superman had ever heard of the games the boys of my generation used to play two score years ago."[12]

Interestingly, the contemporary advice offered by two Columbia Teachers College authorities in *The War Play Dilemma: What Every Parent and Teacher Needs to Know* suggests that caregivers, rather than limiting or banning it, should instead "actively facilitate war play." Educators Diane Levin and Nancy Carlsson-Paige advise that such play can allow children to (1) engage in creative play versus imitation; (2) gain control over their aggressive impulses; (3) take a point of view other than their own, distinguish between fantasy and reality; (4) work out an understanding of what they have heard about the world around them; and (5) experience a sense of their own power and mastery through play. The authors note that the fourth possibility—making sense of a violent world around them—remains difficult but necessary. "It asks us to take on responsibility for helping children," the authors conclude, "with yet another 'problem' created by the society at large."[13]

Military play attracted girls as well as boys during World War II. Some of the younger girls even expressed direct military yearnings: "Dear Mr. Roosevelt: I am only a girl, I know, but I can shoot. I won second in a hard-to-win rifle match. I am only fourteen years old. Why can't I do something in the Army instead of staying here at home? I like action." Anne Bellenger, another young teenager at war's start, would wistfully recall years later, "If I had been a little older, I would have joined the navy. I always felt left out because I couldn't do my part for the 'war effort.'" Even the cartoon character Little Lulu (never one to be outdone) began dragging a toy artillery gun around when she witnessed a boy flying a toy bomber. In another strip, Little Lulu began leading several little boys in a playful military march, complete with pots on their heads as helmets and wooden swords held aloft, because she too wanted to play at war.[14]

"I want to play too" pleaded the eyes of two little girls, holding hands and standing in the background as they watched their brothers and neighborhood boys setting up a complicated game of toy soldier. This small drama, portrayed in a Midwestern newspaper photograph, clearly presented the dilemmas little girls across the country faced regarding their war play during the days and years of World War II. Could they, should they, play war games? Strict gender roles, as determined by well-meaning adults and children themselves, often restricted girls to the sidelines of war play or to supportive and healing roles such as Women's Army Corps and nurses. Girls, however, craved the soldierly drama of defense. As the *New Yorker* cartoon caption countered, "Alice can be a little girl Commando in your game, Donald."[15]

Playing army was a consistent choice for war play with such impromptu game variations as foxholes, commandos, espionage, dive-bombers, and tank battles. Toy soldiers remained a popular wartime item but suffered in production numbers from lead rationing; plastic, wood, and even cardboard replicas had to stand in for priority materials. *Good Housekeeping* promoted one creative kit that used rubber forms for "plast-modeling" soldiers as well as sailors, Marines, and pilots, and therefore a child could build as large a contingent force as desired. By 1943 a parent could purchase complete toy units such as the Fighting Yank Soldier Set for $1.98, which contained "sixteen soldiers in field dress, each with his own type of weapon—a repeating rubber band rifle—a cloth mess hall with table and benches—2 army tents and 6 cloth tents—a movable flag on pole." As the advertisement promised, "Each soldier has useful military information printed on his back."[16]

Isolationist senator Burton K. Wheeler of Montana once used toy soldiers for politically dramatic purposes in the year before the United States entered the war when he staged for his fellow senators a "little exhibit" of miniature soldiers, guns, and searchlights. Wheeler explained that with these particular props he wished "to demonstrate that the British, while requesting war materials from the United States, were simultaneously wasting that metal on toys." The senator believed that war materials sent to America's allies through Lend-Lease were wasted instead on toys and other abuses.[17] After the war began, senators had greater worries than foreign toy soldiers.

Senator Wheeler may not have consciously wanted to begrudge foreign children's small pleasures, and the children's plight would be sympathetically illustrated by the British Relief Society's 1941 Christmas gift coupon campaign. "It looks like a bleak Christmas this year for thousands of boys and girls throughout the British Isles," the campaign reported. "The manufacture of toys has given way to the production of needed war materials. Candy is practically unobtainable. But you can help!" To aid British children: "Each dollar paid for these coupons provides an assortment of toys, games, candy, and other aids to make Christmas a little merrier."[18]

Relatively few toys would be manufactured in England or other war-torn countries, but all children still held some desire to act out war play, resorting to playing with overturned chairs as bombers or broomsticks as rifles. The few toys manufactured in England could, however, seem dangerously realistic such as a board game titled "All Clear," in which players tried to avoid such incidents as falling incendiary bombs or gas attack alerts. Sometimes children in occupied or bombed countries dangerously and realistically tried playing with discarded weapons, bomb casings, and bullet shells.[19] During World War II, only American children had the luxurious option of receiving various kinds of manufactured military-style toys.

In the battle zones as well as in the world of toys, planes grew in importance during the war years although the wooden toy replicas often seemed simplistic versions of an increasingly complex technology. Again, *Good Housekeeping* offered a creative solution for this rising passion despite wartime shortages. "Enemy planes, cut out of luminous paper that glows when the lights are turned out," the magazine promised. "Pasted on the ceiling, they enable the junior 'air-raid warden' to go plane spotting in the dark of his own room. Really exciting!" The kit offered by the magazine also included a civilian defense manual for "young wardens." Price: two dollars.[20]

Amounting to a $25 million business, model airplanes remained a legitimate and popular hobby in the United States, and some miniature mechanized replicas contained engines that could reach speeds of almost one hundred miles an hour. At the beginning of the war, the Department of Education (within its newly established Schools for War program) developed a federal model aircraft program in 1942 with a goal of 6,000 schools, 8,000 instructors, and 300,000 youths participating in the project. These clubs, experts proclaimed, would not only increase community knowledge in accurate plane sightings but could enhance knowledge of aeronautics and serve as initial training centers for the air services.[21]

"I am too young to join the armed forces," Raymond Viola from Brooklyn wrote after listening to President Roosevelt's 1942 Columbus Day speech. "I and the kids in my class are building airplanes models. . . . Although I am only ten years old I buy war stamps and put my money in all the funds and I was one of all the American citizens that helped to

YMCA boys with toy airplanes. Courtesy of the University of Hawaii Archives.

bring in scrap, and we are going to win and nobody can tell me different, we'll keep on flying." Raymond signed his letter, "A Real American."[22]

While airplanes represented the new technological face of war, seagoing ships continued to symbolize traditional military power and might. Because President Roosevelt had a well-known passion for the Navy, a polio-stricken four-year-old boy, leaning on his crutches, carried a toy warship as he ceremoniously approached Mr. Roosevelt during the president's official birthday party in 1942. This birthday celebration was part of the March of Dimes fund-raising campaign for polio research and hospital care. So concerned was this charity about its ability to raise money during an era of wartime priorities that it altered its rhetoric to "fighting a war on polio for children." A military analogy had even entered this equation.[23]

Other toy vehicles of war—jeeps, tanks, and PT boats—also proved to be popular presents throughout the war years. Action and motion remained fascinating components for children of all ages, yet the particularities of design were essential elements of these replicas. Activities such as model shipbuilding also presented teaching opportunities. As the Marine Model Company explained, no better way existed to understand a ship than building a model like the destroyer escort or the liberty ship. Cost: four dollars.[24]

Real military vehicles especially captivated children with their decals, treads, armaments, gears, and sheer size. As a fund-raiser in Washington, D.C., the Army set up an array of equipment—an actual armament display arranged like a playground—at the base of the Washington Monument to encourage participation in the Third War Loan Drive. Dragging their parents along, children thrilled with the opportunity to touch real machines of war, and one little girl dressed in a sailor suit playfully climbed aboard a "half-track antiaircraft height-finder carrier." As the multitude of children interacted with these life-sized "toys," a *Life* reporter captured the excitement: "With the wartime zest of kids all over the world, they swarmed over fieldpieces, tanks and jeeps, pretending to fire big guns and ride roughshod through hordes of Nazi soldiers."[25]

Although only "an infinitesimal amount of metal" was authorized by the War Production Board for toy production, some new manufacturers tried to skirt the rules by not filling out the appropriate WPB forms. Breaking all wartime production rules, one new toy gun's design reportedly contained one and a half pounds of metal. A number of established and legitimate toymakers completely switched their business to war supply contracts to maximize profits, further diminishing a limited toy production compared with prewar amounts. Sadly for this generation of children, just as the toy supply or "store-bought" treasures became scarce, parents now had more disposable income to spend for toys since working- and middle-class parents found themselves with greater discretionary household income for the first time since the onset of the Great Depression. As two boys in a holiday cartoon quipped, "This ain't no time to be cynical about Santa Claus—what with Pop drawing a lot of overtime and Mom earning a buck and a half an hour as a welder!"[26]

Toy loan programs had begun earlier in some Depression-era communities, and although the programs became quite popular and reportedly alleviated juvenile delinquency problems, successful management required adult time and investment, now in short supply. Secondhand, renovated, and homemade toys would still have to appease many childish desires for action, drama, and fun. One Midwestern boy probably considered himself very lucky as he played with toys that his military father had constructed from salvaged plane parts in New Guinea.[27]

"Coasting along easily on velocipede ball bearings," described *Popular Mechanics* in October 1944, "this sidewalk Jeep will be the pride of any boy when he goes out on 'reconnaissance patrols.'" Composed almost entirely of wood, including the wheels, this jeep's design solved part of the wartime toy dilemma of rationed resources. Another wartime vehicle, the "Duration Pump Car," had a purposeful design based on "metal priorities." Parents could purchase cardboard soldiers, tanks, forts, trucks, and trains as well as wooden PT boats with mounted machine guns as toys without metal parts. Unrelenting, the Treasury Department continued to suggest that parents make children's gifts more attractive by attaching war bonds to the homemade toys while explaining to the children that iron, steel, copper, zinc, and rubber were now consigned to real battlefields.[28] Logical, practical wartime intentions, however, probably did little to comfort crushed hearts at holidays and birthdays, and so children might still wish in vain, make substitutions, or sacrifice beloved objects. War bonds always remained abstract; toys were real.

During these rationing years, various board games made simply of paper and perhaps wooden pieces more easily met wartime production standards, and these games became popular with older children who could now became "armchair generals" by playing Air Combat Trainer. Homemade versions flourished as well, and *Popular Mechanics* produced several board game designs for children such as the Military Chessman Maneuver on War Map, complete with a WAC for the queen; Battle Wagons, which placed the Yank at Hawaii and the other player at Japan; or the Grenade Dart Game, which promised that boys could have a lot of fun "tossing wooden hand-grenade darts or 'pineapples' at enemy objectives."[29]

Teachers and parents often regarded books as better "shields" from the topic of war, but children could fulfill military desires with such titles as the Junior Air Raid Wardens, Sailor Jack, or Soldier Sammy. Since toys remained scarce but money was more plentiful for many American war workers, children's books provided a much more acceptable gift than war bonds. As *Life* commented, "Dear Mr. Santa Claus: In case you're worrying about the scarcity of metal toys, we'd like to inform you that the market is flooded with beautiful books for children, which make delightful Christmas presents, colorful and educational too."[30]

Comic books, however, accounted for three-fourths of the leisure reading of children between nine and fourteen, who also spent approximately two hours a day listening to the radio. "Children of today are a degenerate race," declared an editorial in the *New York Times* in November 1941, "when it comes to light reading." What was becoming of America's children? By 1943, more than 20 million comic books circulated each month with such popular titles as Superman, Dick Tracy, or Mandrake. During the war, 95 percent of boys and 91 percent of girls read comic books, but children were not the only audience. The second distinct consumers of the relatively new medium were military men. "Comics were a powerful psychological force," the psychologist Mauricio Mazon notes, "in redirecting the anxieties, anger, horror, and frustration of wartime uncertainty." Another researcher believes that wartime comics could convey all at once "patriotism, chauvinism, and optimism," which might have motivated both GIs and children "to want to do their best."[31]

As varied and vocal protests from parents and educators escalated, comic books only grew in popularity. One reason remained simple: at only ten cents apiece, many children could buy them independently. *Parents* magazine counterattacked by issuing its own series, True Comics, in April 1941. The advertising for the new publication promised parents it would be "a comic magazine your children will love" but also one that parents could "conscientiously encourage them to read." The first cover included drawings of air warfare, frontier fighters, and Winston Churchill. The cost was kept at a dime, and the pages were printed in full color. But could True Comics become a true substitute? Some critics believed it only "sanitized" the comic book format and therefore would never capture children's imagination or the market. Still, True Comics persevered. The August 1945 cover revealed an interesting and thought-provoking split image of recurring world wars versus lasting peace.[32]

While reading might encourage wartime imaginations, replica military uniforms dramatized another dimension. Only in America could adults afford—economically and emotionally—to costume their children in miniature military dress and purchase play instruments of war. Wealth and distance from the conflict provided materials and motivations that perhaps permitted this childhood fantasy. Pretend uniforms for both boys and girls abounded in advertisements, and by Christmas 1942 the headlines in *Parents* magazine proclaimed "Military Fashions Lead Christmas Parade." The available array of children's almost-authentic uniforms allowed adults—in an unusual way—to romanticize the war through their costumed children. Providing a picture of patriotic boyhood, for example, two little boys from Des Moines posed in toy uniforms, holding BB guns and standing in front of a photo of their hero, General MacArthur. Even babies could dress in uniform, and sometimes parents posed their infants next to real military items. At the time, these images of toddlers in military dress seemed only terribly cute and sentimental, not distasteful or downright disturbing.[33]

Large department stores such as Abraham and Straus in New York City offered children's versions of military clothing, reasonably priced. These "hits from Toyland" included, for the little WAC, an official hat, blouse, skirt, and insignia for $2.29. The complete Navy WAVE uniform cost slightly more at $2.89. The little soldier's uniform came with a Sam Browne belt, and the complete ensemble cost $2.29. As the advertisement assured parental customers, each uniform used official colors and durable fabrics for authenticity: "Put your child 'in training' with these official looking playsuits."[34]

Portraying the world of play uniforms with more severity, *Life* later noted that the armed forces had "conquered the world of make-believe" when "pretend" uniforms became available in sizes 2 to 14 of WACs, WAVES, soldiers, sailors, Marines, and aviators. Even cartoon figures enlisted in the military milieu such as Little Orphan Annie organizing a pretend division of the Junior Commandos. "To look like them," Annie explained to her child readers as well as to adults, "takes uniforms."[35] A homemade version of a little WAC uniform is in the Iowa Gold Star Military Museum near the actual WAC training camp at Fort Des Moines. The tiny uniform bears actual buttons from a real woman's army uniform, complete with homely, military-like brown leather shoes.

In search of her own uniform identity, a five-year-old girl applied to enlist at the Spars headquarters, but she received a disappointing rejection due to "an age deficiency of fifteen years." In order to compensate the young girl's display of energy, initiative, and patriotism, the manufacturers of regulation Spar equipment produced a special small-sized uniform. "Anticipating a deluge of requests by other little girls," the commanding officer felt compelled to announce that the quota for "Junior Spars" remained soundly filled, although they were still looking for "older girls."[36]

Another envious little girl named Roberta Fyler had diligently watched and memorized drill formations for a month from her hotel window, and the local military training unit awarded her a specially tailored khaki uniform with stripes and the rank "Little Corporal Pig-Tails." "It's uncanny," said Captain Verne Kasson, commander of the little corporal's unit, the 581st Technical School Squadron, "but she does everything right. She knows all the drill formations and snaps out orders like a veteran top-kick."[37] During the war, play and reality seemed dangerously intertwined.

A year after Pearl Harbor, a War Production Board order further restricted metal for use in toys. "Toys this Christmas won't be made of what they used to be," *Newsweek* reported. The newest toys marketed for that second wartime holiday season were the Super Ack Ack Gun, the New Commando Repeater, and the Recono Peep Scooter. Other toys included canvas army tents, wooden model fighter planes, and plastic replicas of fighting ships and freighters. Two more Christmases with increasing shortages of basic materials would follow. As a columnist for *Successful Homemaking* acknowledged, "While children, too, are conscious of the war, they still anticipate the holiday customs we cherish and their eyes still dance when they see the lighted tree."[38]

But those children who received newly designed war toys throughout these years of global conflict were the lucky ones. Thousands of Japanese American children taken from their West Coast homes to ten internment camps throughout the West were not as fortunate, having to leave most, if not all, of their toys behind. The camp newspaper would later advertise mail-order wares. That first Christmas of 1942 included a variety of nonviolent toys for sale, such as dolls, sewing kits, tea sets, stuffed animals, wood vehicles, and musical rattles. One retailer labeled itself "Santa's Headquarters Toys" with the plea, "Hurry! Buy for the kiddies."[39]

Not one military or war toy, however, was ever offered by merchants or made by parents in the internment camps. For the incarcerated Japanese American children, anything representing aggressive or warlike behavior was officially banned for the duration, even during playtime, and "aggressive adults," by camp officials' definition, found themselves immediately transferred to the Tule Lake Camp in California. At the Tule Lake orphanage, the younger boys played marbles, baseball, and sometimes a game called capture the flag. Ironically, Japanese American boys, just like American boys across the country, would run around yelling at one another, "Kill the Jap."

Despite official camp rules, the children could not contain their enthusiasm for war, especially since a number of boys and girls had brothers who fought in the 442nd Regiment, a segregated Japanese American unit. Children, as resilient as ever, persevered at the internment camps, determined to play on their own terms despite the many harsh rules. If one looks closely at a sketch by an artist confined at the Heart Mountain camp, one can detect in a small group of children the rebellious little boy holding a board much like an Army rifle, despite the possible consequences from security guards stationed in a security watch tower.[40]

Children broke other restrictions as well, although the camp was intimidating to most adults with its circle of nine watch towers, armed guards, and searchlights. Still, no matter the environment and the possible consequences, children needed to play. Wanting to go sledding one cold day, thirty children got outside the Heart Mountain fence that first winter of 1942 but were ordered by the military police to "freeze." The sledding party was arrested and taken in. The oldest of the arrested children was eleven.[41]

In the 1942 poem "Letters from Camp," Margaret Sangster told the story of a very different type of camp—her son's ordinary children's summer camp now closed for the war.[42] But in the opening phrases, Sangster poignantly expressed that surprising and slightly disturbing constancy of children's wartime play.

> Your toys were always soldiers off to battle
> And painted ships and tiny dime-store planes—
> Your baby hands would never clutch a rattle;
> You had no time for wagons or for trains.
> A wee tin hat, a gun, a sword to flourish,
> A tank to draw behind you on a string—
> These were the toys you liked . . .

And little children's play, as this poem from the *Saturday Evening Post* illustrated, could also remind adults of their own need to laugh, even in the midst of a dangerous world war.[43]

> "Eddie's Role" by B. Y. Williams
>
> When you are a little boy,
>   Only two,
> What the big boys say
>   Is what you have to do.
> Eddie looked so small
>   Squatted on the ground
> While the sticks and the stones
>   Rained all around.
> I called to the big boys,
>   Luther and Jim,
> Perched in the tree
>   On an overhanging limb,

"This won't do;
  Shame on you!"
But the answer came
  With Yankee vim,
"He's Tokyo.
  We're bombing him."

Play, however unusual it might have appeared to adults, remained children's tangible way of coping with the abstract situation of a violent world at war, as the following passage from *Through the Eyes of Innocents* illustrates:

> As the summer of 1945 drew to an end, most American boys had left their backyard battlefields. Mothers heard fewer and fewer shouts of Bang! Bang! You are dead!" under their kitchen window. The boys had finally put down their Red Ryder BB guns and were busy at work in garages, sheds, and basements. On September 2, 1945, six years after the outbreak of World War II in Europe, and three weeks after Nagasaki was destroyed by a nuclear blast, the *New York Times Magazine* published an article that related the experience of a curious mother who went to see what activity had replaced the game of war. She found her son and his pals fabricating a strange contraption out of tin cans and flashbulb lights. When she inquired what project they were working on, the boys told her they were making an atomic bomb![44]

The postwar period also presented difficult play scenarios and equally troubling times for its "baby boomer" generation.

5

Soldier Citizens

Vigorous Youth
Increase in Production
Competency in Math and science
Total use of manpower
Overcoming inflation
Realization of the Air-Age
Your part in the fight for freedom

—Virginia's school program in *Education for Victory* (December 1942)

Eleven-year-old Truelove Timms entered the Los Angeles hospital shortly before Christmas Day 1941 for a tonsillectomy. Not only did the hospital seem like an entirely new world to this little girl (a young migrant worker who could pick 147 pounds of cotton a day), but the gifts from the hospital staff seemed amazing to her as well. A new doll. Toys. Truelove had never had shoes or stockings let alone her own doll, but due to the escalating wartime economy, migratory workers now had jobs, and her parents hoped to emerge soon from their complete poverty. Cotton would be king again, proclaimed the *Los Angeles Times* in early 1942, though racism and classism remained part of the migratory agricultural economy, exemplified in another photograph of a child cotton picker and the demeaning newspaper caption: "all happiness of the South seems to be reflected in this grinning pickaninny picker." Along with wartime employment, racial discrimination also rose higher and higher.[1]

"It is significant that tomorrow—Christmas Day," began President Roosevelt in his 1942 Christmas Eve radio talk, "our plants and factories will be stilled. On all other holidays the work goes on—gladly—for the winning of the war. So Christmas becomes the only holiday in the year." The president realized that workers had earned a day off from their defense jobs. The labor shortage during the Second World War remained intense and could be filled only "by every capable man, woman, and child stepping forward." "Teach them that there is no Santa Claus," the federal journal *Education for Victory* informed American teachers, "that we will get no more than we work for, and that unless we work hard enough and intelligently enough we shall be worse off than we could ever have imagined."[2]

Work—at all times and by all citizens—was essential if the United States were to win this war. To be "the arsenal of democracy" required stamina and numbers. The year 1942 began with a *Parents* magazine cover illustration of three children portrayed as young soldier citizens, standing straight and proudly saluting. Paul McNutt, director of the War Production Board, wrote "National Defense Begins at Home" for *Parents* early in the war because he believed that children would be called upon to work in a variety of strenuous ways for the war effort. "We have learned from our own experience of recent months," McNutt concluded, "that defense exacts a heavy price from youth." By June 1942, *Parents* was directing American mothers and fathers to prepare their children to fill all sorts of jobs that were rapidly developing in response to the war emergency.[3]

With more than 2.8 million teenagers employed in agriculture and industry by 1943, the ever-increasing numbers of children at work startled even those adults who became actively engaged in their recruitment. Approximately 500,000 older teenagers worked in vital defense plants, and 580,000 under the age of sixteen labored in other types of positions. Thirty-four states allowed teenagers at the age of fourteen or fifteen to legally leave school for work. Initially, Americans viewed this desire to work for the war cause positively and even romantically such as an acceleration of the American work ethic reconfigured as "the Teen Age Reconversion." For example, when the Lockheed plane factory hired 1,500 boys at the beginning of the war for riveting, assembly, and sheet metal work, managers discovered that two boys working four-hour shifts were often more productive than one adult on an eight-hour shift. The numbers proved efficient, and *Life* named the phenomenon "Boy Power."[4]

Labor issues had been a growing feature of factory life during the Great Depression, but as Shelton Stromquist notes in his oral history of World War II, two labor conditions changed with war production: unemployment was replaced by labor scarcity and the federal government desperately needed uninterrupted production. Factories had to produce without fear of strikes or employee shortages that might slow the war effort. Popular opinion during the war, as the historian William O'Neill describes in *A*

Democracy at War, was strongly negative about labor issues such as strikes and agitation for higher wages or safer working conditions because of the desperate need for war production. But as he also points out, no one seemed to question farm or business profits related to war production. David Hinshaw in his book *The Homefront* believes that although labor remained highly patriotic, the unions still argued—though sometimes faintly—that the wartime era must not jeopardize labor's recent gains. Veterans needed to return to a fair labor environment.[5]

Labor scarcity challenged the standard composition of the industrial labor force. According to historian O'Neill, 15 percent of America's workforce remained "idle" as late as 1940, but unemployment totals in Iowa, as one example, plummeted during the war years, from 95,088 in March 1940 to 17,000 in November 1944. With increased employment opportunities, the labor force itself changed. By the spring of 1945, the national labor force exceeded the average number by 7.3 million, of which the largest new groups of employees were 2.8 million teenagers, 1.9 million women over thirty-five years old, 1 million retirement-aged men, and 600,000 young women with servicemen as husbands. New war workers from less traditional employment pools, though, remained highly vulnerable at war's end, and discrimination lingered in hiring practices as expressed in a 1941 lyric "Defense Factory Blues."

> Went to the De-fense factory
> Trying to find some work to do,
> Had the nerve to tell me,
> Black boy, nothing here for you.[6]

The Des Moines Ordnance Plant, similar to other defense factories around the country, initially resisted hiring local black workers, arguing that white opposition to black workers would cause slowdowns. But the full-employment economy of the war challenged the outdated management "preference" for white male labor, and African-American leaders recognized the opportunity for old barriers to finally fall.[7]

An early challenge presented to the Des Moines Ordnance Plant's policy came from an eighteen-year-old black woman. Elizabeth Shackelford had been recently named by the National Youth Administration after a war training program as "youth worker most valuable for war production" for a ten-county region of Iowa. In April 1942, she brought suit in federal court against the U.S. Rubber Company because the company "refused to employ [workers] in the capacity for which they are best qualified." She called this a violation of President Roosevelt's June 1941 executive order, which alleged that discrimination became harmful "in spirit and practice by delaying the defense program." Nationally, Shackelford's was the first lawsuit of its kind.[8]

The intent of the case was to draw attention to discriminatory hiring practices and, perhaps, to change these practices for the good of the war effort. Reporter John Coleman had made a number of visits to training centers and war industries in Des Moines for the *Bystander*, a newspaper that served the black community in Iowa. At first he found widespread discrimination, but, as he later commented, "present opportunities are improving." The Des Moines Ordnance Plant did improve its hiring practices, and black Iowans eventually held 4 percent of the plant's jobs, a ratio that matched the 1940 black population in Des Moines. According to historian Daniel Nelson, two factors accelerated the movement of African Americans into industry: one, Roosevelt's executive order, and two, the agitation of union groups that favored "an inclusive approach."[9]

In early 1942, when Americans felt the war effort was not going well, defense employment discrimination became an issue of national concern. Many Americans believed that every effort should be made to improve war production while avoiding practices of discrimination, and skilled black leaders spoke out on the issue. Lucile Bluford, editor of the *Kansas City Call*, campaigned diligently for black Americans in war production. Bluford saw blacks making progress against discrimination and even nonwar industries opening their doors, but she believed major discrimination still lingered. The realization that the war was not going well could actually bring positive changes. "We are losing in the war," Bluford observed. "America has to change in a hurry her attitude toward color."[10]

Other ordnance plants began to set better examples. The St. Louis Cartridge Plant employed three thousand blacks in all roles from supervisory to unskilled. The Hercules Powder Company in New Jersey hired a thousand black workers, and the Wolfe Creek Ordnance Plant in Tennessee held a ratio of 20 to 25 percent black employees. More black Iowans continued to find positions at the Des Moines Ordnance Plant, which placed notices in the *Bystander* during subsequent labor shortages. By war's end, the company was advertising prominently in the black community's newspaper yet ironically displayed discriminatory wages by gender: men received 68 cents to $1.03 an hour while women's hourly wages remained at 54 to 78 cents.[11]

Middle-aged women doing their bit for the war effort as "Rosie the Riveter" certainly contributed to the remarkable home-front war production effort, but teenage boys and girls solved war's "manpower" shortage in far greater numbers. During World War II, America's proportion of child labor reversed its previous downward trend and began rising rapidly. In 1940, employed children between fourteen and seventeen numbered 1.7

million; by 1944 this figure had grown to 4.61 million. The number of mill girls alone rose from 271,000 to 950,000, and overall 1.8 million boys and girls under eighteen labored strenuously on farms and factories.[12]

Not wanting to leave teenage girls out of a potential employment pool, Representative Margaret Chase Smith, one of only a few female members in the House during World War II (Smith would be elected as the first female senator in 1948), proposed as early as August 1941 to change war's labor laws to allow girls under the age of eighteen to "work under contract to the U.S. Government." Boys from sixteen to seventeen possessed the legal right, and early in the war employers had fired teenage girls in order to take on new federal contract work for war supplies. In November 1942, the federal government lowered the required age for girls employed in war industries from eighteen to sixteen except in hazardous factories such as ordnance plants. As one older teenager eager to work in the Oregon shipyards commented, "We were ready to do some war work, something more exciting than typing."[13]

The labor crisis crisscrossed the continent. In Oregon, twenty thousand boys and girls, fourteen to eighteen, drew industrial paychecks at a rate of sixty-five cents an hour. As early as 1941, North Carolina issued ten thousand new labor certificates to seventeen- and eighteen-year-olds and a thousand work permits to twelve- to fifteen-year-olds. "The situation," state labor commissioner F. H. Shuford sarcastically observed, "is as healthy as the war that brought it on."[14]

Teenagers working in factories for the war effort met mixed community reactions of pride and concern. Between 1940 and 1944, the national school enrollment of fifteen- to eighteen-year-olds fell by 1.2 million or 24 percent, while the number of employed fourteen to seventeen-year-olds increased by 2 million or more than 200 percent. During the war years, the employment rate of fourteen- to fifteen-year-old girls jumped by four times along with heavier workloads and hours as many adolescents dropped out of school altogether during this period.[15]

The psychologist Anna Wolf suggested in *Our Children Face War* that the "Youth's Share" in the war effort needed to center on motivations of patriotism and citizenship, but American educators and employers strongly believed that this patriotic desire to serve should not transform American children into some perverse version of the Hitler Youth. Accidents were another concern. According to a 1943 article in *Collier's*, "Children for Hire Cheap," many children, some as young as ten, appeared caught up in this youthful craze for earning, often with little consideration for safety.[16]

The Second World War not only renewed patriotism and the work ethic but also emphasized materialism and the youth culture. The two values seemed in conflict—the traditional work ethic versus the modern value of

A boy working in a cannery. Courtesy of the State Historical Society of Iowa Archives.

education. As developmental specialist Alma Jones perceived the conflict, some "reconverting" after the war might be needed to get teenagers back to school; otherwise young people with little formal education would not be able to compete professionally, especially against veterans with the advantage of the G.I. Bill.[17]

The character of factory work itself was positively transformed during the war years. When workers became the soldiers of production, taking a factory job became a patriotic action, not a socially demeaning one for many adults. Children carried even fewer stigmas and filled all sorts of jobs, especially routine service positions as well as housework and child care, which relieved adults to work in defense plants at a higher rate of pay. A sampling of jobs for children included delivering newspapers, minding siblings and neighborhood kids, tending soda fountains, stocking grocery shelves, operating telephone exchanges, and assisting nurses. All work appeared positive during this era because all ages possessed a fear of idle hands.[18]

The media coverage of children's work ran the spectrum from the saccharin to the grotesque. Scott Tissue pursued a series of ads throughout the war years in which illustrations of toddlers bore the captions, "What can I do?" or "I want to be drafted, too!" The answer was to pick up toys and clothes as well as carry dishes and trash, all with a cheerful smile: "You can be a Wartime Clean-Up Warden." At the other extreme, children were assigned rat killing duty as farmers "enlisted" them as allies in their war against vermin. The declared champion rat killer was Robert De Glopper, age seven, of Grand Island, New York, who turned in eighty-three rat tails at three cents each to earn $2.49.[19]

Younger fry simply wanted to "get in there and pitch"—"a need to feel needed"—as a formal part of the nation's war effort, but as educators often reminded the public, even during war a balance needed to be struck. By the beginning of the second school year after Pearl Harbor, employment had given teenagers a sense of serving their country. "Their experience has given them a keener sense of what life means," began the *Education for Victory* statement. "That sense they should not lose. But, at the same time, they must not lose sight of the fact that they have a mission in the future and that their current work is not the whole answer for themselves or for the Nation."[20]

Predicting "a lost generation of youth," Robert Lynd, famous coauthor of *Middletown* and professor of sociology at Columbia University, warned that the boys and girls now employed would soon be losing their jobs to returning veterans, emerging as a generation "too young for the glory of having been in war and passed over when jobs are given to returning veterans." Lynd also predicted angry times ahead. "In spite of optimism, philanthropy, and youth conferences," he emphasized, "this is one hell of a world for kids to be trying to grow up in, with the situation deteriorating, not improving, as power politics on a world scale and fear and cynicism here at home increase." The work and the times were far more complicated than could be alleviated by simply "pitching in." "Youngsters are concerned about the war," said Robert Sears, head of the Child Welfare Research Station at the State University of Iowa, who advised "that they want to do something tangible to help, but they must be guided in their efforts."[21]

"It won't be long before planting will be going strong," wrote Ruth Elaine, editor of *Successful Farming*'s "The Playhouse." "You'll probably get right out there and help like the fine little Playfellows you are." The *New York Times* offered a similar message that winter of 1943: "Boys—and girls—play an important part in achieving the farm production goals which will feed ourselves and Allies." All agreed that children's labor was necessary on wartime farms, but the ideal and the reality of their working conditions conflicted. The ideal was a picture of children working on their family farms, a vision of healthy, disciplined, even educational tasks conducted in the great outdoors with plenty of fresh air, bright sunshine, and wholesome food. The reality of children's work in the midst of World War II, however, often consisted of long hours, tiring labor, repetitious tasks, dangerous conditions, little if any compensation, and lost time from formal education.[22]

Still, at the beginning of this global conflict, the United States faced a tremendous military challenge with few organized resources, and in truth, America desperately needed the labor of her children to produce the necessary food. "Food is a weapon" was the constant refrain. "Sometimes a farmer, alone in the field," as *Wallaces Farmer* explained, "fails to see the army which marches alongside him, the army of six million American farmers who this year are breaking records, reaching new goals."[23]

Immediately after the United States' official entrance into the global war, the emphasis on farm production swelled in response to recognized worldwide deprivations. Food for Freedom was instituted as a coordinated federal campaign to produce less of the traditional agricultural products and more of those crops and animals needed by the armed forces and America's allies. "Farmers the country over are producing food for freedom," *Wallaces Farmer* encouraged, "food for our armed forces, food for our factory workers, food for our fighting allies, food vital for victory, food to win the war and write the peace, food in ever-increasing amounts to feed the hungry of the devastated and ravaged lands as they are liberated."[24]

Increased agricultural production required additional labor just at a time when farms across America were losing their traditional supply of older sons and hired hands to the armed forces and war industries. The military branches offered pride of service and the factories presented larger paychecks—two temptations difficult for young men to resist after experiencing little opportunity for either during the Great Depression's decade. But how could the nation fill this new labor void?[25]

"Labor is the number one problem of Agriculture in 1943," *Successful Farming* noted. With so many young men leaving for war or industry, approximately 2 million replacement "farm hands" were needed nationally. Military deferments for young farm hands or older sons helped to stem the tide of this labor loss, but mostly older men along with women worked even longer hours to satisfy Food for Freedom's production goals. Ultimately most farmers realized they must turn to other sources of labor, especially their children.[26]

The work remained unrelenting each year of the war. Shortly before the approach of D-Day, farmers still felt uncomfortable with the media's overdone analogies of farm field to battlefield, or of soldiers tilling the soil with soldiers hitting the beach. "Don't Praise Us Please," pleaded farmers through *Wallaces Farmer.* "After New Guinea or Cassino, the rush of spring work seems flat," commented an anonymous Iowa farmer. Work continued day and night on the farms—dramatically under moonlight, electric lights if available, even blazing corn stalks. "Mamas and grandpas, school boys and girls, do all the chores except those which Dad is particular about, and these he sandwiches in himself," *Wallaces Farmer* said. "Almost unbelievable progress was made by long hours on tractors, labor of women and children, help of town folks and doubling up on machinery. There were shortages of labor, machinery and sunshine, but no shortage in the will to produce another good corn crop."[27]

Throughout this continuing war work, few farm families ever felt sorry for themselves. "Almost everybody I know is working harder, playing less, sharing more, and enduring more irritations than usual. That's war!" explained Joseph Davis, author of a Stanford University Food Research Institute pamphlet. And a poem appearing in *Successful Farming* that first wartime Thanksgiving captured the poignancy of the multiple expectations of all family members during this wartime agricultural crisis.[28]

> "Thanksgiving 1942" by Grace Noll Crowel
>
> This is a different year from other years;
> We sent our sharp plows deeper in the sod,
> Driven by desperate need and anxious fears,
> Craving a closer partnership with God,
> That we, too, might be soldiers in the fight
> For justice, freedom, liberty, and right.

Children certainly felt the tension and wanted to help their parents in all sorts of chores. Ruth Elaine, coordinator of "The Playhouse," received hundreds of rural children's letters each year, detailing in childishly scrawled sentences the importance they placed on their farm work. "Thanks for your letters telling me what you have been doing to help with the war effort this summer," Elaine commented. "I'm sure your brothers, uncles, and friends must be very proud of you. When you multiply what you have been doing by what thousands of girls and boys all over the country have been doing, it must be bad news for the Axis!"[29]

Children helped fill this unrelenting agricultural labor vacuum. Although issues of war remained clouded and confusing, the expectations of work could be straightforward and praiseworthy—a concrete approach to an abstract situation. Children worked on their family farms in ever-increasing hours and tasks: sawing wood for the stove, pulling weeds, collecting eggs, slopping hogs, planting and husking corn, cultivating beans, cutting grain, making hay, harvesting oats and wheat, milking cows, watering calves, driving tractors, repairing fences, washing dishes, canning fruits and vegetables, cutting and threshing oats, plowing, disking, harrowing, and spreading manure. And after wiping the mud off their shoes, washing their hands and faces, eating their dinner, perhaps reading and doing their homework, these farm children across rural America fell to sleep—only to perform their early morning chores before catching the school bus or walking to their country school.

Historians agree that farm children's labor remained a central, necessary component in the survival of family farms until the end of World War II. As child historian Viviana Zelizer notes in *Pricing the Priceless Child*, while factories became associated with an exploitative version of children's labor, family farms maintained an image of "good" agricultural work. Still, as historian David McCleod observes, children's farm work did not follow a modern middle-class emphasis on education, play, and volunteerism. As historian Pamela Riney-Kehrberg critiques, "Need often dictated the balance between work, school, and leisure. Work was at the center of farm children's existence." Even three- to five-year-old children could contribute on the farm during the war years. And the new work regimen wasn't seen as necessarily ending with the war. "This training needn't be just 'for the duration,'" the *Iowa Farm Bureau Spokesman* explained. "Self-reliance, independence, and consideration of others are valuable character traits in peacetime as well as under war conditions."[30]

Although sons and daughters were the first (after farm women) to fill the labor shortage in agriculture, organized groups of farm children through their clubs and schools made further contributions. Nationally 4-H considered itself to be an army of 1.5 million members, and more than 241,000 FFA members lived in 7,300 localities. In 1943, Kansas farmers enlisted the labor of 25,000 Boy Scouts.[31]

But still more children were needed. *Wallaces Farmer* posed this question to Iowa farmers: "If you were assigned a city girl to help on the farm, where would you employ her? In the field? In the kitchen?" Nineteen percent of the farm men supported the idea of "land girls" in the field, 38 percent considered the kitchen appropriate, and 43 percent remained undecided. Those undecided farmers, the surveyor quipped, probably meant that they "couldn't think of any place where a 'land girl' would be

A teenage girl working in a bean field, 1943. Courtesy of the New York State Archives.

any good at all." Only 10 percent of farm women supported using "land army" girls in the field, but 59 percent favored the kitchen while 31 percent remained undecided. "It doesn't require any mechanical training to wash and wipe dishes or scrub the floors," as one farm woman in Washington County put it, "but I think these 'land army' women would have a hard time running a tractor. And no farmer has time to teach them." A doubtful farmer from Jones County said, "If I have to have a woman helping me in the field, I want my wife, not some green city girl."[32]

In New York, one answer to the farm labor dilemma became the Farm Cadet Victory Corps. One hundred Girl Scouts from New York and New Jersey aided farmers during harvest time in Ulster County after their peace-time summer camp was converted into "a farm aide stronghold." "The girls got pretty tired the first day," their camp organizer reported proudly, "but none of them missed the bus the next morning. They're gathering a fine crop of freckles and making a contest of their work."[33] In the fifth edition of their camp newsletter, *Farmerette Fanfare*, one girl penned the following lyric:

Thanks for the memory
Of aches and pains received
Of how we've been deceived—
Fresh air and exercise
But if we are not wise
We ache from feet to eyes
Thank you so much
Thanks for the memory
Of fields all green with beans
And oh those awful scenes.[34]

In a message from the Girl Scout Council, President Harriet Popkin reported on another aspect of the Farm Cadet program. "This is the third year of a great experiment at Camp Tivoli," Popkin chronicled. "Girls from all walks of life have banded together to replace the fighting men who have left the farms. Our job is not easy. Few of us have had any experience in farming; some have never been to the country before. There are inconveniences we city dwellers are not used to. Most of us are used to privacy; some, to pampering. But we're learning how to take this in our stride. We're in the 'land army' now!" She continued, "We want teenage girls everywhere to know that this is one of the biggest contributions they can make to the war effort. We here at Tivoli are glad to be able to do our share." The pamphlet attempted to encourage and enroll these young farm workers and emphasized the group's purposeful motto: "I want to help keep hunger from the shores of America."[35]

New York City boys certainly responded positively to this call for farm labor. One example of eagerness came from a Brooklyn boy named John Monaco. "Me and few other boys heard about going to a farm in the summer," John began writing to New York's agricultural officials, "and we would appreciate very much if you could have us sent up in the summer we can carry many things and we would like to go but we would like very much is you send us the details and where to go and where please answer this letter to the fowling address (Brooklyn) on the bottom I will give you the age and almost correct height." Farm Manpower director T. N. Hurd personally responded to these New York City boys with the promising comment: "We shall need thousands like you to help harvest the food we need to win the war."[36]

Fred and Richard Higginbottom behind their father's tractor, 1945. From the author's personal collection.

New York learned to ask its citizens directly for young farm help. In a radio ad from the New York State Division of Commerce, the narrator began:

> I want to talk to all high school boys and girls throughout New York State! Here's a grand opportunity to do almost as much for your country as your older brothers are doing in the armed forces! A chance to do hard, healthful, interesting work on America's farms! A chance to help win the important battle of food! Today with so many farm workers away at war and working in defense factories, America needs your help to prevent the threat of hunger to her armies, her allies, her people.

Governor Thomas E. Dewey concluded the radio promotion with his official endorsement: "If you are in high school now and over the age of fourteen, join the Farm Cadet Victory Corps of the State of New York. I urge you to enroll with your teacher tomorrow, subject to your parents' consent!"[37]

The Farm Cadet Victory Corps program provided for teenage students to be released from school somewhat early in the spring and to live and work individually or in pairs as hired farm hands for most of the summer. From

1942 to 1943, the program grew from fifteen thousand to twenty thousand young workers, and organizers raised the proposed age limit from fourteen to sixteen because of the overwhelming response from city children. Younger children now excluded by the new rules strenuously protested.

> I am fifteen years old and am willing to work on a farm during the summer, but a notice was sent through my school (Erasmus Hall High) saying that in order to go to the farms, it is necessary to take a farming course given in a nearby high school. In order to take this course, you must be at least 125 lbs, and sixteen yrs. of age by September 1943. Can't anything be done about this situation? There are many other boys of my age who are willing and capable of doing the required labor and who are in the same predicament.[38]

Young Marvin Gedaly from Long Island City refused to give up his farming dream. He wrote three postcards to Governor Thomas Dewey beginning with the normative details: "I am a boy of thirteen who will be fourteen in July. I am considering going to the farms this summer but I have no information on the Victory Farm Corps. Please send me all the necessary information on the work, pay, etc., and blanks for my parents signature." After Marvin received the standard official reply from the governor's assistant A. D. Gentle that he should visit his principal, this determined boy wrote again: "I have done this and he informed me that I would have to be sixteen I would have to pay my first two weeks board and that my parents would have to take out insurance for me . . . but in a speech on the subject he said applicants would have to be only fourteen." In a third note, Marvin persevered, "I am writing you again as a last resort. I have hounded my principle so often about the farm that I am bared from the main office. . . . If you can help me in my plight I would be extremely grateful to you."[39]

Another fifteen-year-old boy named Walter—six feet two inches tall, strong, healthy, neat penmanship—also wanted to volunteer for the Farm Cadets but was slightly underage. Walter pleaded his cause in a letter to Governor Dewey: "The ruling is that a boy must be at least sixteen years old by September. I therefore take the liberty of asking you if you could help me to get a job on a farm this summer, so that I will be able to help my country in a time of need." Perhaps financially pinched parents were behind notes such as these.[40]

Farmers had reasons to be grateful for the children's help. After the ending of the 1944 harvest season, 641 New York farmers (from a total of 1,730) responded to a formal survey regarding the youthful farm assistance. Of those responses, 55.7 percent replied with an excellent review of the boys' labor records, 22.4 percent felt just "all right" about the program, and 21.5 percent marked it "poor." The teenagers had performed more than 75,000 "man" days of work that season. Some of the farmers offered personal comments and suggestions such as asking the program directors to pay "particular attention to attitude as well as physical characteristics" of the young workers. Other farmers emphasized the need for "an orientation training for the purpose of tempering possible useful enthusiasm by stressing the realities of work on a farm and living in the country" and "emphasizing the obligation undertaken to follow through a job." Camp operations within the state ultimately consisted of twenty-five harvesting work camps with 2,500 young people in attendance from one week to three months.[41]

A national program called Victory Farm Volunteers was designed by the Office of War Information to recruit high school students, and the Department of Education promoted this labor program through its wartime journal, *Education for Victory*. The Agricultural Department's extension director, M. L. Wilson, reported near the end of the summer of 1943 that the program had placed in suitable farm employment more than 138,000 boys and girls by July and 500,000 children by the end of the season.[42]

Rather than placing youth on individual farms or bunking them in junior work camps, another child-oriented labor strategy was the "day haul." In the summers of 1943 and 1944, a "day haul" of children from Buffalo, New York, assisted with the harvesting of berries and beans in the area. Parents, farmers, and even educators agreed to lower the age limits for this agricultural program to twelve and a half years for boys and thirteen for girls. "In conversations with parents we find that many prefer to have their children doing supervised farm work rather than remain in the city during the long summer vacation especially where both parents are employed," explained T. N. Hurd. "The farmers have definitely expressed a desire for some of the younger children. Very often they are a much steadier source of labor than the 'high school' age boy and girl."[43]

Children working in the fields seemed preferable, at least to parents and farmers, than children roaming about the streets. As children labored in fields and in barns during these difficult war years, some controversy emerged over the number of school hours that rural children should also spend in school. Although public schools remained "geared to war," certain ideas needed to mesh. Yes, in the short term an emergency need for farm labor certainly existed, recognized by agriculturalists as well as educators. But in the long run, this loss from education might never be regained. "Since Pearl Harbor," as the teachers' journal *Education for Victory* stated succinctly, "many students have been leaving the classroom, sacrificing their education to take part in the war effort."[44]

National educators concurred that although small alterations might be made in the educational schedule, overall most farm youth should remain in school. In his radio address of October 1942, President Roosevelt praised the Victory Farm Volunteers but stressed "this does not mean closing schools and stopping education." Roosevelt perhaps believed in an idealized agricultural world from his youth at Hyde Park along the Hudson River, but he had gained more realistic perceptions from his long stays at rural Warm Springs in Georgia. "A summer's work on the farm has high educational value for town and city youth," the president noted. "Rural life is especially suited for the development of such qualities as acceptance of responsibility, readiness to take the initiative, reliability, healthy attitude toward work."[45]

Roosevelt's words echoed an earlier initiative proposed in *Education for Victory*: "During the summer several million high-school boys and girls have worked on farms, in factories, in stores, and offices. They have gained valuable work experience. They have helped to supplement family incomes. But most of all, they have felt that they were helping to serve their country." Educators now believed that a combination of work and school might best suffice for high school students eager to earn a paycheck. "Their experience has given them a keener sense of what life means. That sense they should not lose," proposed another *Education for Victory* editorial. "But, at the same time, they must not lose sight of the fact that they have a mission in the future and that current work is not the whole answer for themselves or for the Nation."[46]

This dangerous craze of work hours in defense factories had also affected those in farm fields. With children working increasingly longer hours on their family farms, the risk of injury and even death from farm accidents intensified. The seven machines that caused "the great bulk of deaths and permanent injuries," according to *Successful Farming*, remained the tractor, combine, corn picker, corn elevator, corn sheller, corn shredder, and circular saw. In 1940, machines and animals killed more than two thousand people on the farm—even before the greater wartime effort with its corresponding accidents. *Successful Farming* and other agricultural periodicals continuously warned their readers, especially those concerned with children's safety, of possible scenarios: "John did better with his combine, but he never forgot the day his four-year-old was playing in the field up ahead of the sickle and almost got threshed."[47]

Risks on the farms remained despite precautions. "This spring and summer a lot of youngsters will run tractors for the first time," *Wallaces Farmer* warned. "But unless we are careful, too many of these boys will be hurt before the season is over." The magazine concluded at the end of the summer of 1943, "Weariness and a wide spread of responsibilities sharpen normal risks. Poor judgment, physical frailty and hurry are often the start of disaster. Child injuries frequently result from adult negligence." Youth organizations took the lead in teaching farm safety such as a new booklet titled "4-H to the Safety Front," which advised that "every preventable farm death and injury constitutes an unpatriotic waste of our human and material resources and hinders the speed and effectiveness of our war preparation."[48]

Wartime conditions brought dangers, stress, and exhaustion but also pride in the accomplished labor. The following two poems from a mimeographed newsletter of the Tivoli Camp illustrate the range of new farm experiences for urban girls who had worked "on the land" in upstate New York during the course of war:

"Fields and Orchards"

Working in the fields each day
picking berries, pitching hay,
thinning apples and picking weeds—
from knees to ladders, from fields
to trees.

The sun is hot upon my back
as I walk barefoot on the land . . .

—M.L.

"Sunstroke"

Picking strawberries row by row,
Making ever so little dough
Breaking your knees, ruining your nails,
Tearing your clothes—who cares?
no males!

—Ethelyn Snarck[49]

A supervisor of a New York girls' farm labor camp attempted to explain the girls' demanding wartime contributions. "One of my duties was to visit the girls on the farms at work," Geraldine Suydam reported. "I marveled at their conscientious effort despite the terrible heat." Children in the "Black Dirt Region" struggled under particularly stressful conditions, and Suydam asked that other Americans consider what these girls had contributed to their country's war effort.

> The heat was intense, the black dirt clung to every fiber of their bodies, and I have given first aid to girls whose legs were badly burned

> from kneeling on the black dirt to pick the onions. The strong aroma of onions was seething through every inch of them, but they still continued on their job. I have talked with many of the farmers, and the majority of them prefer the girls to men in certain types of work; because they are willing to do many jobs that men consider too menial.[50]

By war's end, America's farm youth easily deserved some overdue praise. In recognition, chief of the Agricultural Education Service W. T. Spanton produced a special broadcast on June 8, 1945. "To American farm youth," Spanton said, "together with a large number of overage farm operators, farm women, and girls who have worked long hours, day in and day out, must go a great share of the credit for our tremendous agricultural production during these war years."[51] *Successful Farming*'s children's page editor also praised her young and devoted readers who "have truly helped to fill the nation's breadbasket." The chorus of "Hail the F.F.A." sang only of optimism.

> We're the lads who turn the furrow
> And our faith is in the soil
> We are building, ever building
> For a brighter farming day.[52]

Yet concerns lingered. Had the children's time, energy, commitment, patriotism, and duty—created, encouraged, and maintained by parents, teachers, work force directors, and government officials—been overwhelming and unethical? An *Iowa Farm Bureau Spokesman* article in July 1944 had the courage to finally state, "Youth's labor cannot be exploited in the name of patriotic necessity."[53]

Other worries made family farmers apprehensive. "How would high school boys, who had been the big men of the farm and the neighborhood, like it when big brother came home and took charge?" At farm women's meetings, the ladies' talk by the end of the war years turned increasingly to other concerns, about "where their boys are" and "what they heard last" because far too many farm families were grieving for older sons sent from farm fields to combat zones. "To such families," *Wallaces Farmer* poignantly noted, "the post-war problem isn't hog prices or egg prices or anything else in the economic field. It is how to live without Jim."[54]

6

War Waifs

War like every other human ailment tends to leave the body politic folded along ancient creases and festering in old sores.

—W. E. B. DuBois, "A Chronicle of Race Relations" (1942)

To be a *nisei* was to participate fully in American life—school, church, sports . . . "to eat Wheaties and drink Ovaltine." Yet it was also to be told and treated as if you were irredeemably different.

—Lauren Kessler, *Stubborn Twig: Three Generations in the Life of a Japanese American Family* (1993)

"Have you ever lain awake on Christmas Eve," asked a child of the internment camps, "with everything about you strange, quiet, and still as death?" As Christmas drew nearer, the older children at the camp realized that gifts and attention and fun would be in short supply, so a small group decided to decorate the mess hall with red and green crepe paper and wreaths of desert holly. A young child praised the effort for the first Christmas behind barbed-wire fences: "As if with the waving of a magic wand, the bare cold mess hall was changed into an enchanting place."[1] For a few moments, a holiday celebration would be cherished and the fear of "military necessity" diminished. Most of the children felt very far from home.

For Americans, the war meant movement. The Second World War dramatically redistributed the United States population more than any other historical moment, and in the three and a half years after Pearl Harbor, almost 15 million citizens changed their resident county. In December 1944, the President's Committee for Congested Production Areas published a list of overwhelmed regions, which included eighteen cities in fourteen states. California headed the list with 782,705 new residents in Los Angeles and 514,815 in San Francisco, but 254,485 Southerners, black and white, had moved to Detroit, Michigan, as well. By war's end, one of every five Americans had participated in this great war migration due to the decentralization of newly established war industries. More than 8 million men, women, and children moved to other states, usually in a pattern of south to north, east to west, rural to urban. America's towns and cities boomed.[2]

Children might be left behind with relatives in their home towns, but most boys and girls traveled with their parents to new defense jobs and rather defensive communities. There the struggle began. Most boom towns did not welcome, much less prepare, for most of their new adult residents, but certainly children complicated the exploding formula. Assessing initial war conditions on the home front, Samuel Grafton found a Connecticut airplane engine factory's community, for example, that had "little use for children." One father with ten children had to distribute the siblings under six different roofs, including those of public institutions and relatives, in order to find adequate housing. "If you are a Hartford worker and have a new child, you hide it," Grafton described the tense circumstances. "Should the landlord see the young one he will say 'It!' and raise the rent one dollar a week. Or order you evicted. Fifty-five families were evicted in April for the crime of having children."[3]

No laws protected children from housing discrimination. "Should landlords bar children these days?" asked a new migrant worker in frustration to the *Los Angeles Times*. This anonymous worker had tried for days to find housing for his wife and five-month-old baby, but no landlords would rent their vacant properties to parents—"doing much to hinder the war effort."[4]

As a new inspector for a St. Louis war plant, William Scheid received two hundred rejections from potential landlords because he had four children. Desperate for lodging so he could keep his new job, Scheid sent this poem to the local newspaper:

> Children, they say, are heaven-sent
> But to have them means you cannot rent.
> I've done my best, as has my spouse
> But, to save our soul, we can't find a house.
> Landlords, it seems, were born full-grown,
> Or so you'd think to hear them moan;
> But surely somewhere there must be a few

That also love little children, too.
If one of you should see this ad,
Rent us your house and you won't be sad.

The poem apparently pulled some heartstrings, and within days Scheid's family had several "fine offers."[5]

Federal government projects sought to meet the housing challenge in some overstressed areas. In Bridgeport, Connecticut, construction began in 1943 on garden apartments to house more than two hundred families in salmon-colored brick duplexes, complete with garages, playgrounds, and nursery schools. This type of project remained exceptional. Most migrating families in booming communities nationwide found themselves in worn and crowded—even squalid—rentals or makeshift trailer parks.[6]

Many African American families in Chicago, Cleveland, Philadelphia, and New York, according to the historian Darlene Clark Hine, lived in substandard, segregated rentals—overcrowded, poorly ventilated, and vermin infested. In Chicago, according to the report by the Mayor's Commission on Race Relations in 1944, more than 11,160 one-room apartments housed two to six people each, and many of Chicago's African American families lived in one-room kitchenettes. Often three to five families shared apartments originally designed for single families but now divided into even smaller units. Another report that same year by the Metropolitan Housing and Planning Council described these arrangements as "far below the minimum mandatory for healthful sanitation." The novelist Richard Wright describe one of these units "with its filth and foul air, with its toilet for thirty or more tenants, which kills our black babies so fast that in many cities twice as many die as white babies." Cecelia Donald, a teenager during the war, remembered living with two other families in a two-room kitchenette in Chicago. She washed in a tin washtub, and although everyone "took turns cleaning," nothing seemed to alleviate their "rotten living conditions."[7]

The summer of 1943 became as "long, hot, and troubled by racial strife." Conflicts between black and white residents broke out in Beaumont, Texas; Los Angeles, California; and Mobile, Alabama, but Detroit became the scene of the most notorious race riot of the Second World War. Life in Detroit was characterized by strict segregation in its social practices and discriminatory employment patterns, and housing conditions remained crowded and overpriced. By 1943, Detroit's population was more than 1.6 million of which 210,000 were African Americans; recent migrants from the South included 35,000 blacks and more than 500,000 whites. War meant movement, but hostility often traveled along the way.

Two "Junior Commandos" on a scrap drive collection route in Roanoke, Virginia. Courtesy of the FDR Library and Archives.

On Sunday, June 20, 1943, the temperature in Detroit reached over 90 degrees. Bitterness and anger long in the air exploded near Belle Island where many migrant workers had gone to escape the heat. During the night, rumors heated up, claiming a black woman and her baby had been thrown from the bridge. Jackie Smith Arnold remembers the rioting that ensued. "On Monday, as the fighting drew closer to our neighborhood," he recalled, "we were released early from school and directed to go straight home." The children were specifically told not to use the passenger tunnel under Cass Avenue, directly in front of the school. "Safely home, we sat in our third-floor window and watched while a white gang chased a black man in one direction; then a few moments later a black crowd chased a white man in the other direction. In my childish mind I thought they were taking turns." Anthony Volino also remembered feeling scared and confused. "As a ten-year-old, I felt apprehensive about the fighting," Anthony recalled. "As a defensive measure, I placed a couple of baseball bats at my front door to ward off any threat."

The riot eventually required federal troops to restore order to Detroit, and Jackie Arnold also remembered playing near the troop headquarters. "We played around the tents," he explained, "and the men treated us as if we were their own children or their younger brothers and sisters." The official death count at the end of the rioting was thirty-four residents, black and white. In a democracy fighting fascist forces, the racial chasm seemed immense.[8]

"The Grand Canyon of the mechanized world" was Charles Lindbergh's description of Willow Run, Henry Ford's newly constructed bomber plant less than an hour's drive from Detroit. A bomber could be built completely within the mile length of the factory. Lindbergh elaborated on the factory's magnificence: "The glare of the machinery and the polished aluminum and the clouds of dust made it impossible to see its whole length." Willow Run was considered by industrialists to be "a monumental construction feat."

But not until six months after production began at Willow Run would the family units for its workers be completed on a site nicknamed Bomber City. Most new workers had lived and continued to reside in shacks, tents, and trailers with little running water and no laundry facilities. New school construction also remained far behind schedule, resulting in overcrowded classrooms on half-day schedules. The Willow Run bomber plant—with 43,000 new employees—became a technological marvel but a social disaster; the previously sparsely populated region was unprepared and often unwilling to meet the sudden demands of workers' housing and particularly family living arrangements.[9]

In December 1943, Senator Claude Pepper of Florida traveled with other congressional committee members to one of the major "congested areas" in Pascagoula, Mississippi, a defense area considered to be "Willow Run in miniature." The Ingalls Shipbuilding Corporation had transformed this town from a prewar population of 4,000 to 30,000 by 1943. The senators sadly discovered that children's basic needs suffered most as doctors and day-care centers remained in short supply, and elementary schools split into two shifts to accommodate migrant children.[10]

Racism, according to Midwestern historian Beverly Russell, was often "casually accepted," as illustrated by a Nebraska schoolteacher's description of her town's rapid population changes: "With people moving in from everywhere, there were Indians, colored people, and oh, so many kinds of people living at the trailer camp near the fair grounds." More than 700 trailers were quickly situated in the ironically titled Pleasant Hills Trailer Camp in Hastings, Nebraska. Native American, African American, and Mexican children would now be attending school together, but the schools were overcrowded with 47 percent more students in 1943–1944 than the year before. Some classrooms even had fifty-seven pupils. Administrators extended the school day into shifts and hired extra teachers, creating further strains on an already tight educational budget.[11]

Portland, Oregon, would become another boom town described as "cautious and localized" in its social style as "We Cater to White Trade Only" signs still appeared in local businesses. Despite President Roosevelt's executive orders to prohibit discrimination in defense industries and government programs, racism persisted in Portland's housing. In September 1942, more than five hundred residents (including parent-teacher groups) participated in a meeting of the Central East Portland Community Club to protest "the further influx of negroes into the area" because "they already constituted a menace to the neighborhood."

When the Kaiserville housing project, later renamed Vanport, was constructed in August 1943, the workers' new residences were characterized by "shoddy construction, overcrowding, deteriorating roads, and inadequate public services." Shortly after the war in 1948 when a dramatic flood struck the area, Vanport's 18,500 black and white residents found themselves forced to evacuate and find other housing, especially difficult for poor black residents who faced continuing postwar discriminatory practices.[12]

Wartime migration often demanded rapid movement with little preparation and few resources: "neither easy nor painless" as John Gurda writes in his examination of Milwaukee industry. After the Great Depression, both communities and incoming workers became eager for abundant jobs and an influx of money—paychecks, business transactions, and tax revenues. Still, families worried about their ability to stay together. Times might be tough, but at least wartime sacrifices seemed productive, progressive, and patriotic.[13]

Wartime migration offered a few choices; internment offered none. For more than 110,000 Japanese Americans, leaving their homes was not voluntary but mandated. On February 22, 1942, President Roosevelt signed Executive Order 9066, which established ten camps for West Coast Japanese Americans located in Wyoming, California, Idaho, Colorado, Arizona, Utah, and Arkansas. Sixty-three percent of the internees were American-born citizens, and more than a quarter of those evacuated were second- or third-generation children under fifteen years of age.

These concentration camps (as originally labeled) were organized by the federal government soon after the Pearl Harbor attack out of anger and fear, but they also represented older local animosities and jealousies toward Japanese immigrants. Children who were not of Japanese ethnicity remembered being surprised by the sudden violence their parents displayed after Pearl Harbor, as mothers and fathers hurled names at the new enemy and destroyed toys and china. As William Tuttle learned when people who had been children during World War II wrote to him of their experiences, they had ugly memories of that first month of war. "Some children," Tuttle discovered, "stood helplessly as their enraged parents smashed to pieces any toys 'made in Japan.'"[14]

Fear pervaded all of the United States but especially the West Coast. Sumi Utushigawa, a young teenager living in Los Angeles's Little Tokyo district at the time of Pearl Harbor, remembered standing "motionless at the window" as she watched "Anglos" swarm her neighborhood streets "looking to see if Little Tokyo's Japanese were celebrating their homeland's attack on the United States."[15]

Rural areas were also vulnerable to outbreaks of hostility. "I was helping on the family farm," as Oregon teenager Mikiso Hane remembered his first hearing of Pearl Harbor. "I had just learned to maneuver the Farmall tractor and was spreading fertilizer on the field all day that Sunday. It wasn't until after five that I went home. That was when I first heard about the Japanese attack on Pearl Harbor. My reaction was one of shock . . . and then fear about what public reaction toward us would be like." For Japanese American citizens growing up in California, Oregon, and Washington, racial bias and discrimination had represented, as Mikiso commented years later, "facts of life that we had been conditioned to live with since childhood."[16]

Although the anger and nationalism prompted by the war were the overt reasons for establishing the internment camps, agricultural competition and economic jealousy were other factors. To circumvent anti-Asian immigration laws, many Japanese Americans had built successful farms and businesses by purchasing land in their children's names. In 1942, approximately 25,000 of the 40,000 acres of truck farms in Los Angeles County were owned and operated by Japanese Americans—a thousand farms—but by April much of the land had been taken over by the government and private owners after the federal internment removal process. For example, Gardena Valley High School students began planting beets that spring on ten-acre plots of land previously owned by Japanese Americans. As a sad ironic twist to this agricultural confiscation, Californians predicted and lamented an early wartime strawberry shortage due to, as the *Los Angeles Times* phrased it, "Jap Farm Evacuation."[17]

The internment process began in certain regions in March 1942 and would be completed by summer's end. At age seven, Peter Yoshida remembered traveling by train with the blinds pulled down along the entire route to their assigned camp. "They said it was for our own protection," Peter recalled. Heart Mountain, near Cody, Wyoming, was a rapidly constructed mountain camp with rows of numbered barracks, barbed wire, spotlights, watch towers, and subzero temperatures. Harshness was directed even toward the children residing within the camp's gates. "The soldiers guarding us were ordered to shoot if we even tried to retrieve a ball outside the fence," Peter remembered. "While some people harbored resentment about all this, I didn't. I was young and was told, 'War is war.' I did, however, wonder why we were singled out."[18]

Dressed in his Cub Scout uniform, ten-year-old Norman Mineta boarded a train to "the assembly center." Ironically Norman had participated in Boy Scouts for years because his parents had wanted him to integrate quickly into American society. Now the uniform appeared meaningless. Later that year, even the *Los Angeles Times* commented on "the strong Americaness" of the young evacuees who appeared during the evacuation process wearing "the nondescript garb of American high schools."[19]

Within the internment camps, parents strived to create as normal a childhood as possible for their sons and daughters. In Heart Mountain's community, a "Children's Hour" began in November of that first Wyoming winter, in Barrack No. 22–26. Mothers scheduled the weekly event from 10 to 11:30 a.m. for preschool children to sing American songs, hear Bible stories, and work at various crafts. The Community Christian Church planned a toy drive for the residents' first "white Christmas," and several toy companies advertised collectively as "Santa's Headquarters" to parents in the *Heart Mountain Sentinel* with tea sets, stuffed animals, wooden toys, musical rattles, and dolls. Even though the newly formed community tried to create a "Happy New Year," its newspaper noted that the ten thousand Heart Mountain residents greeted 1943 with "mingled feelings."[20]

Besides holiday celebrations, clubs remained another avenue toward creating normalcy for children in the camps, and the Boy Scouts, Girl Scouts, and Camp Fire Girls proved particularly popular. A "Recognition Ceremony" was planned for that first Christmas season at Heart Mountain complete with candlelight to honor nearly eight hundred girls in Girl Scouts and Camp Fire Girls. Girl Scouts also enjoyed hiking and camping in the local hills, promoting war bonds, and selling more than two thousand boxes of Girl Scout cookies.[21]

Boy Scouts not only sold war bonds and stamps but earned merit badges and participated in hiking trips to nearby Yellowstone National Park. Wyoming's Boy Scout executive leader M. L. Johnson declared Japanese American boys and girls to be "as American as Apple pie" as he countered local residents' complaints regarding Boy Scout internee trips during gas rationing. "These Scouts were not on 'pleasure trips,'" Johnson argued, "but part of an Americanization program deemed 'completely successful.'" Boy Scout troops usually met three times a week in the Japanese schoolyard, learning helpful skills such as safety and handcrafts as well as marching and drilling. The Boy Scouts' motto at Heart Mountain would be widely

A little boy's Victory garden. Courtesy of the University of Hawaii Archives.

shared throughout the other nine camps: "Toughen up, buckle down, and carry on to victory."[22]

Young second-generation Japanese American students before and after Pearl Harbor saw themselves simply as Americans. As Karen Riley notes in *Schools behind Barbed Wire*, the events following Pearl Harbor were shocking to "many of these youngsters who, until then, believed that their citizenship status and ardent patriotism protected them like an invisible cloak." School became a central part of their new life in the camps with attendance increasing at Heart Mountain from 850 elementary students in 1943 to 980 students the following year. Teachers and classrooms offered a normal routine to school-aged children's lives. Although classrooms might be makeshift—cold, dusty, temporary, poorly furnished—the sparse and confined quarters did not keep children from participating in the "miracle of learning." The internment camp schools' stated purpose, ironically, was to "promote understanding of American ideals and loyalty to American institutions."[23]

Victory gardens took a different turn within the internment camps. At Heart Mountain, a two-thousand-acre victory garden was created in "the Midst of Desert," led by the Issei (first generation, often sixty years or older men) who used irrigation techniques, manuring, cover crops, and hotbeds to create remarkably productive plots whose produce supplied the other internment camps. In fact, the ten camps together cultivated more than ten thousand productive acres of gardens from previously idle land in "a true pioneering effort," and produced all the vegetables (along with beef and poultry) needed for the 93,000 Japanese American residents. In 1944, NAACP director Roy Wilkins commented (with a statement that almost branded him a Communist by the FBI) that Japanese immigrants had been "the best truck farmers in America."[24]

Heart Mountain became an organizational triumph, emerging as the third largest city in Wyoming during World War II. As in every American community, blue and gold stars hung proudly in many family windows, honoring their young men's military service. Heart Mountain alone had 150 blue service stars with thirty-five young men who had volunteered a year or two before their relatives' incarceration, and by February 1942 more than 5,000 men of Japanese ancestry had enlisted in the U.S. military.

The camps had been quickly converted from abandoned racetracks and isolated, marginal land. When Carey McWilliams, California's commissioner of immigration and housing, visited an internment camp that first year, he believed his earlier advocacy for migrant workers would have prepared him for the stark living conditions. Still, McWilliams described his first sighting as "an extraordinary experience." An American Civil Liberties Union (ACLU) member noted on his first official visit that he "just wanted to cry." As McWilliams later commented, "Those who knew individuals whose lives were uprooted and whose loyalty was impugned simply because of their race were not inclined to believe the idea of 'military necessity.'" White children would also recognize the unnecessarily grim circumstances. Erica Harth was the six-year-old daughter of a WRA worker at Manzanar and the only Caucasian child in her first grade. She recalled, "On the flimsiest of pretexts, ten thousand people were jammed into the small plot of land that made such a puny prison cell for them, and such a large playground for me. The meanness of the space measures the enormity of the injustice."[25]

"Mo's Scratch Pad" had appeared as a weekly column for the *Heart Mountain Sentinel* written by a young Nisei woman named Miwako Oano. On a June evening in the midst of war and slightly more than a year after evacuation orders, Miwako composed the following essay titled "Proud Thoughts" in which she reflected on camp life.

> Walking around camp the other day after dinner, I got to thinking about certain things. It was one of those cool evenings when the breeze is soft and cool and little-flat-bottomed clouds, puffed with dreams, hang from a baby-blue sky. One of those evenings just made for a quiet, "thinking" walk.

The people in here now are displaying by their daily living, a courage and fortitude I would not have been able to imagine on the outside.

Walking along, I passed old folks bending over their victory gardens or sitting in the shade of home-made porches, quick to respond to my smile. I passed children laughing and quarreling at play—shooting marbles, spinning tops, pitching ball—just as I used to see children playing on the outside. I passed young couples strolling hand in hand, an air of silent happiness bubbling about them, and I passed tired but able-looking police wardens on their beats. From a distant baseball field, cheers and laughter, muffled by the wind, reached my ear and all at once I was overwhelmed at the awful immensity of evacuation and the human sacrifice and drama enveloped in it.

Only a very great or weak people, I thought, could have submitted with so little protest to such a movement. And though I may be prejudiced, I believe it takes a people bigger than the sky to keep their faith without rancor as we have done in the face of all that has happened.[26]

A week before Christmas Eve, on December 17, 1944, the War Department announced that the mass exclusion orders for Japanese Americans would be revoked. But leaving the camps would take much longer than expected, and few residents wished to return to their West Coast homes or farms. For Japanese Americans, their internment became "the central, defining experience." More than half a century later, as Lauren Kessler notes, "camp" remained "the single, most important reference point for the entire generation."[27]

If only something larger could be gained from these divisive times, some Americans wondered. Perhaps in a democracy, even one engaged in a vicious world war, its citizens might still learn from each other, maintain individuality, and practice, at the very least, tolerance for difference. Maybe, as George A. Towns would write of such challenged relationships:

> Youth, white and black, no more consent
> To be pushed here and there, tradition's pawn.
> . . .
> Together, standing firm, they face foursquare
> In staunch defense of freedom, full for all.
> . . .
> So shall they be new pioneers
> Of a new world beneath the sun,
> Where men shall learn to banish fears,
> To realize through all the years
> That goodwill never needs a gun.[28]

7

Zoot Suits and Victory Girls

In times of stress, young people feel a pressure to grow up, and all their emotions and personal problems are intensified.

—"Growing Up in Wartime," *Parents* (April 1943)

There is something fundamentally wrong with a civilization that regards a sixteen-year-old as an irresponsible child and at eighteen will take him into the army to face the most drastic tests of character.

—Anna W. M. Wolf, *Our Children Face War* (1942)

A small group of fifteen-year-olds had been skipping school, shooting BB guns at little kids, learning how to smoke, playing a "uke" too loudly, disobeying parents, coming home after curfew (sometimes after 2 a.m.), bothering phone operators with foolish questions, "borrowing" other kids' bicycles, and refusing to do chores. The story sounded fairly familiar for young teenage boys in the early 1940s: occasionally silly, mischievous pranks but sometimes ugly, destructive behavior. The boys were also accused of hanging out in other kids' barracks, sleeping at night in the rec hall, and being "out of bounds" on fishing trips. These were not just any American boys, however, and this was not just any American community. This was "The Trial of Tom Yamoda" in 1944 at the Heart Mountain Relocation Center in Wyoming with Chairman Doi presiding.

Chairman Doi asked a number of direct and harshly phrased questions of the teenagers, Tom in particular, about not obeying their parents and aiming BB guns at little children. "And if you missed the legs," Doi asked, "and hit the eyes, the child may have been blinded, isn't that right?" Tom had also skipped thirty-four days of school the preceding year. The trial continued with the harsh questioning until finally Tom broke down and began crying. The chairman ordered a short recess. When the trial resumed, Doi pronounced his judgment and prescribed Tom's punishment: carry all the coal for the family that winter and study each night for an hour and a half. Doi also strictly admonished Tom to obey his father and mother. "Do your homework," the chairman concluded, "and you may play after you have finished your homework, do you understand that?"[1]

Tom's situation may have been unusual, but his story of rebelliousness and dangerous disregard became more and more familiar during the course of the Second World War. Wartime was "the perfect ground," began a *Saturday Evening Post* article, "for the seeds of juvenile delinquency to grow fast." The editors did not attempt to diminish the issue of juvenile delinquency while describing the efforts of a rookie policeman, a young black man named Oliver Crowen, who believed there could not be "a bad boy." In "a horrific neighborhood" in Washington, D.C., with "the dirt and the smells and the squabbling that send children into the streets to find life and amusement," Officer Crowen remained convinced that these young "hoodlums" and their energy could be directed toward constructive activities rather than culminating inevitably in crime. In his work, Crowen took children who believed they had failed and gave them increasing levels of attention and civic responsibility. "You see," Crowen explained, "many of these kids never had a chance." Under his care, the children now participated in various ways, according to their individual talents, as official members of their own newly created Junior Police and Citizens Corps.

These children had been given a creative opportunity organized by a caring adult leader, but most children in trouble across the country did not have such an advantage. The *Post* editors concluded, "Are we raising another Lost Generation? One of the greatest evils of this war is its sinister effect on the behavior and character of America's children."[2]

"Our kids are in trouble," observed *Life* magazine, responding to a rise in juvenile delinquency that became a serious concern in 1943 and 1944. Across the country, boys were arrested on a variety of charges—train-wrecking, "hoodlumism," willful destruction of war materials and other property, arson, assault, rape, murder. "Many specific cases can be traced directly to war excitement," *Life* reported, "to a misguided (or rather, unguided) desire on the part of underage youngsters to do something as thrilling as their big brothers in uniform." Some boys were becoming "thrill saboteurs" and forming "Commando Gangs." Movie theaters provided especially dangerous opportunities with dark corners and lack of supervision resulting in "rowdyism," vandalism, purse-snatching, fires, and sexual assaults.

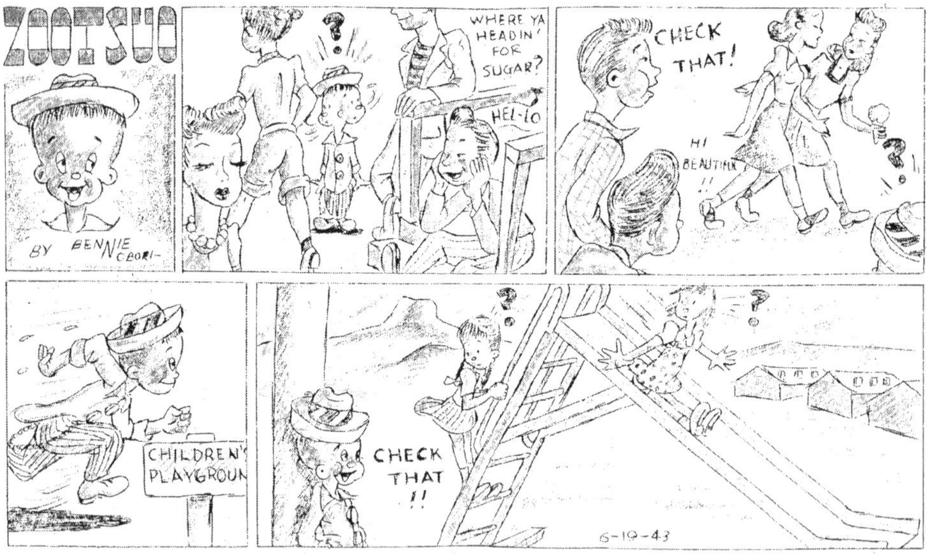

Cartoons from the Heart Mountain Internment Camp newspaper. Courtesy of the American Heritage Archives at the University of Wyoming.

Girls were creating trouble too, being arrested for running away, truancy, petty thievery, vagrancy, drunkenness, disorderly conduct, prostitution, and other sex offenses. "The teen-age girl," *Life* explained, "with a pretty but empty head, and an uncontrolled impulse to share somehow in the excitement of the war, has become a national problem child." Both American boys and girls seemed to be displaying "a distorted kind of patriotism."[3]

The home front presented new social and economic conditions for adolescents, opportunities as well as problems, which startled much of the adult population, and this new unruliness—whether innocent, unavoidable, or malicious—was labeled "juvenile delinquency." Authorities varied in their responses. "Juvenile delinquency is the label," one child psychologist believed, "attached to a mounting series of social maladies directly traceable to the war. Something can be done about it."

The list of factors that seemed to be producing these greater numbers of arrested children in America and other countries at war was extraordinarily complex. Boom towns with racial and cultural conflicts topped the list. The absence of parents and a resulting neglect of children formed a strong secondary factor, but another influence was "flush times," as teenagers suddenly experienced increased wages along with "a moral letdown." This combination of wartime circumstances created a charged atmosphere with a philosophy of "eat, drink, and be merry, for tomorrow we die." Wartime brought to a society additional "habits of violence," but much of the increasing youth crime remained a mystery for most adult authorities. "All we really know about the extent of juvenile delinquency," suggested the Children's Bureau, "is that it has increased in some communities, and that the rate of increase is greater for girls than for boys."[4]

Other experts believed that the chief cause was the eagerness of boys and girls to be a part of the escalating war effort, but this energy and enthusiasm had somehow become misdirected. Growing up, even in the best of times, has always presented difficult choices, but in the worst of times tragedies multiplied. Dr. Gardner and other experts tackled the problem of troubled times at a Harvard conference titled "Tomorrow's Child," hoping to describe and possibly curb this explosion of juvenile delinquency because, as Gardner surmised, youth troubles stemmed from "internal problems complicated by external situations." By 1943, New York City and Chicago had witnessed increases in youth crime of 10 percent while in "boom towns," numbers of arrests often doubled. Curfews such as San Francisco's 10 p.m. for those under sixteen and New York City's midnight rule were familiar but ineffective responses.[5]

Or was juvenile delinquency merely a media exaggeration to sell newspapers and magazines? Broadway responded to this concern or perhaps played into the commercial aspect of deliquency with two plays that portrayed the growing difficulties girls faced in wartime America—girls caught at that liminal age between girlhood and adulthood. *Kiss and Tell,* which one critic described as "a bright comedy of juvenile sex in the suburbs," centered on a fifteen-year-old girl who pretended a pregnancy and dramatized the consequences of this lie for her family. The second play, titled *Pick Up Girl,* featured another fifteen-year-old girl whose troubles began when she met a sailor in Times Square.[6]

Vice and crime, as represented by delinquents, was not the wartime image of its younger citizens that the United States government intended to promote. Rosie the Riveter was the preferred American personification of the ideal war worker. The real Rosie, however, remained far more complicated and less easily tamed for the home front effort than the lyrics of the popular song would admit.[7]

> While other girls attend their favorite cocktail bars,
> Sipping dry martinis, munching caviar,
> There's a girl who's really putting them to shame.
> Rosie is her name.
> All day long whether rain or shine
> She's a part of the assembly line.
> She's making history, working for victory,
> Rosie the Riveter.[8]

Rosie became a World War II icon—the epitome of hard work, perseverance, and unity. She represented the woman working behind the man who went to war to defeat the Axis. Although her image challenged conventional gender ideas with her costume of work pants and kerchiefed hair, Rosie symbolized the dictates of a wartime society. The young American woman asked no questions, wasted no time, and challenged no authority.

Opposite to the wartime ideal, the zoot-suiters—young men or boys of flamboyant dress in Los Angeles, New York City, Philadelphia, and other urban centers—were controversial to the general wartime public. The negative aspects of zoot-suiters (according to their opposition) included dressing in too flamboyant a style, wasting targeted resources, killing valuable time, and opposing both military and law-enforcement officials. "The narcissistic self-absorption of the zoot-suiter in a world of illusory omnipotentiality," psychologist Mauricio Mazon notes, "was in opposition to the modesty of individual selflessness attributed to the defense worker and the soldier." Mazon further explains, "Zoot-suiters transgressed the patriotic ideals of commitment, integrity, and loyalty with noncommitment, incoherence, and defiance. They seemed to be simply marking time while the rest of the country intensified the war effort."[9]

A skirmish broke out in Los Angeles in August 1942 after the murder of a Mexican American teenager, and violent fights escalated in June 1943 for six days that collectively became known as "the zoot suit riots." Mexican American boys and girls—"zooters"—had formed "pachuco gangs," according to the city's major newspapers. That August more than 300 youth, ages fourteen to twenty, found themselves picked up in the largest two-day roundup since Prohibition. Of the 170 arrests, charges varied from violent behavior to curfew violation to drunkenness. "Marijuana cigarettes were sold openly on suburban streets," Sheriff Biscailuz told the *Los Angeles Times*, "and the girls and boys smoke them, get half crazy, and go looking for another gang to challenge to a fight, using knives, clubs, bottles, chains, guns, or any other weapon they can find."[10]

Official explanations of the young people's behavior ranged from rising wartime juvenile delinquency to defense plant discrimination against Mexican youths. Some Americans even believed the riots, labeled "Boy Gang Terrorism" by the *Los Angeles Times*, represented an Axis conspiracy involving Mexican agents designed to sabotage the American war effort, "a divide then conquer their opponents" tactic.[11]

The violent behavior of young men was by no means singular. In the early summer of 1943, American soldiers and sailors grew increasingly bored, tired, and scared as they waited around the explosive and confusing city of Los Angeles to embark on unknown Pacific missions. Sometimes acting in mobs, military men often began the confrontations with Latinos.

"Los Angeles was a microcosm of wartime change," the historian Tom Sitton explains. "The economy exploded as federal munitions orders demanded more factories and workers, including large numbers of women and minority workers."[12] The war's "beehive" of round-the-clock activity at defense plants, shipyards, and military bases created an environment that provided young Mexican Americans with too few resources and generated too much anger in American soldiers. Military men directed their overall resentment at an urban youth in conspicuous clothes, not understanding the dynamics and dangers of the different dress during an era of wartime uniforms especially prevalent in a wartime boom town. As a sixteen-year-old white youth trapped in the middle, Don McFadden remembered, "A lotta people got hurt, a lot of innocent people, a lot of these young Mexican kids."

Who were the zoot-suiters? What was a zoot suit? "Later historians may argue the point," wrote a *New York Times* reporter in June 1943, "but J. V. D. Carlyle, fashion editor for *Men's Apparel Reporter*, seemed convinced that the first zoot suit on record was ordered early in February 1940 at Frierson-McEver's in Gainesville, Georgia." Carlyle noted that Clark

Gable as Rhett Butler in the 1940 film *Gone with the Wind* had appeared in several scenes with the long coat and peg trousers that became staples of the complicated costume.[13]

Other sources thought the zoot suit began earlier in the 1930s as part of an urban jazz ensemble such as Malcolm X's description of his first zoot worn in Depression-era Boston. "I timed myself to hit Roseland as the thick of the crowd was coming in," Malcolm described his first evening out in his flashy new suit. "In the thronging lobby, I saw some real Roxbury hipsters eyeing my zoot, and some fine women were giving me that look." Some fashion experts date the attire back to a previous turn-of-the-century "dandyism." Whatever its origins, the zoot suit caught on among urban working-class young men and boys during the course of World War II, especially the "swing-mad kids" or "hep cats." As a 1942 song began,

> I wanna zoot suit with a reet pleat
> With a drape shape and a stuff cuff
> To look sharp enough to see my Sunday girl . . . [14]

The suit had a long coat (usually well past the fingertips) with exaggerated shoulders paired with ballooned and pegged trousers with hues ranging from bright colors to mad plaids to sharkskin grays. During the war years, a tailored zoot suit could cost from fifty to well over a hundred dollars, but some customers with less cash bought off-the-rack suits four or five sizes too large and had these "draped" in bootleg tailor shops. (In Los Angeles, the zoot suit simply became "the drape.") The zoot suit was known to be quite expensive, depending on the material and the tailor, while an ordinary off-the-rack suit at that time usually cost less than twenty dollars. No zoot ensemble was complete without hair slicked into a "duck-tail" and accessories of a V-knot tie, long key chain, wide felt hat, Dutch-toe shoes, and perhaps a flask of whiskey concealed in the coat.

Not only did the price of the ensemble seem excessive to many Americans but so did the extra material in a wartime economy. The War Production Board ended "jive-garb production" for "teen-age jitterbugs" in March 1942 when it placed limits on cloth other than war production. In other words, no pleats, cuffs, or long jackets. But the wartime ban symbolized more than simple shortages. As Senator Guy Gillette from Iowa, who led the congressional "zoot suit bloc," declared, the young men's suits appeared "scandalously wasteful."[15]

The zoot suit transcended racial and regional boundaries, representing a youthful urban expression. Alice DeNomie, an Ojibwe teenager growing up near Milwaukee, remembered tailoring "fat men suits" in glen plaid with Joan Crawford shoulder pads for her teenage brother and his friends, sharply creasing the pants and topping the outfits with porkpie hats. Alice also recalled the long chains that the boys used to swing while doing their slow walk or "creep" to create the overall persona. The zoot served not so much as a political statement for Alice's family or community as a more confusing squawk of rebellion. Her mother never could understand "why anyone would want to look that comical."[16]

Describing a young man's journey from the Deep South to Harlem's streets, Ralph Ellison in his 1952 novel *The Invisible Man* portrayed the romantic effect of the zoot: "What about these three boys, coming now along the platform, tall and slender, walking stiffly with swinging shoulders in their well-pressed, too-hot-for-summer suits, their collars high and tight about their necks, their identical hats of black cheap felt set upon the crowns of their heads with a severe formality above their conked hair? . . . Walking slowly, their shoulders swaying, their legs swinging from their hips in trousers that ballooned upward from cuffs fitting snug about their ankles; their coats long and high-tight with shoulders far too broad to be those of natural western men." In 1943, Ellison commented in *Negro Quarterly* that opponents hated "the zoot" and the American public "failed to understand it," such as a *Newsweek* reporter who despairingly described the zoot suit as "distinctly something from the bottom drawer."[17]

Young boys and men wore the apparel not only to impress one another but young women as well. Sometimes known as cholitas, Mexican American girls also organized themselves into groups with the self-selected labels of "Slick Chicks" or "Black Widows," as they developed a similar style of rebellion. Girls would at times wear the long zoot coat with pants or short skirts, but usually they conformed more closely to wartime gender expectations. Still, Mexican American girls might wear shorter skirts, tighter sweaters, mesh stockings, and rolled pompadours despite the strictures of family and community, and this provoked attention from military men that disrupted neighborhood communities' sense of propriety and authority.[18]

Zoot-suiters were certainly not representative of all Mexican Americans but sometimes emerged from a group labeled *panchucos*—a second generation of working-class Mexican immigrants who challenged mainstream society with their interest in urban culture and an edgy mix of swing dance and stylish clothes along with occasional drinking and drugs. *Panchucos*, though usually a derisive label, could be either Anglicized Mexicans from Los Angeles or the "underworld" of Mexico and Texas who were reputed to "live a wild life of fighting, drinking, drugs, and sex."[19] Not "good kids," in other words. These *panchucos* and *panchucas* would never be the media darlings like those Boy Scouts or Camp Fire Girls who led community scrap drives or war bond campaigns. Rather, zoot suits were groups or gangs of extremely independent young people, increasingly impossible to control during a time of war.

With its influx of servicemen and defense workers, Los Angeles as a whole seemed difficult to control during the Second World War. While war factory work might be considered patriotic for middle-aged married women of Rosie the Riveter age, the increased hours in the lucrative new job market proved problematic for teenagers. Their employment opportunities prompted rising dropout rates, excessive time away from homes and tightly knit community authority structures, and full pockets of spending money. After so many deprivations during the Great Depression, kids just wanted to find some fun.

"It was a birthday party on a ranch on the outskirts of Los Angeles," began the *Newsweek* article. "Guests caught a dozen Mexican boys and girls of late teen age stealing beer and chased them away. But the youths returned shortly with reinforcements and armed with tire irons and knives." One young Mexican American man, José Diaz, would be found severely beaten in the bushes outside the party, and he later died at a Los Angeles hospital. The account in the *Los Angeles Times* reported, "One killed and 10 hurt in Boy 'Wars'" as "a grisly toll from juvenile gang warfare."[20]

After José Diaz's murder, local police officers made more than three hundred random arrests. The various felony charges against the youths included offenses such as robbery, suspicion of assault with a deadly weapon, violation of selective service regulations, violation of curfew, drunkenness, and suspicion of burglary. "Revolvers, knives, crank handles, rocks, and toy pistols," reported the *Los Angeles Times*, "were held as evidence by police." The murder at Sleepy Lagoon resulted in twenty-nine zoot-suiters going to trial.[21]

The press never recognized the long-term consequences of the vigilante reaction for these vulnerable boys. As the *Los Angeles Times* headlined two months later, "Ten Zoot Suit Boys Trip Gayly Out of County Jail in Error." The reporter, perhaps trying to be too clever, revealed other aspects of society's disdain: "Ten zoot suit boys did a zoot scoot from the County Jail last night, where they were booked on suspicion of assault with a deadly weapon—but it was all a mistake." The reporter turned from jaunty to derogatory with this supposed dialogue: "'Theese ees wunderful, ees eet not, Pedro?'" said one of the youths, as they were called from their cells and sent merrily on their way." Accusations that the press had been biased and inflamed the crisis would live on in the 1981 play titled *Zoot Suit,* which recounted and elaborated many of the discriminatory events during those two Los Angeles summers.[22]

Los Angeles did not stand alone in the outbreaks of violence. In San Francisco, servicemen mobbed twelve zoot-suiters; in Philadelphia, white youths beat up four black zoot-suiters; and in Detroit, sixty-five zoot-suiters (also wearing white armbands) attacked a group of high school boys and stabbed one. Many causes, many stories. As a *Newsweek* reporter wrote, "But all sides agreed on one thing: The sight of a young man in a zoot suit in wartime was probably enough to infuriate many servicemen." The final tabulation in Los Angeles amounted to six nights of fighting, nine civilians and eighteen servicemen treated for serious injuries, and ninety-four civilians and twenty servicemen arrested. Five civilian youths were injured for every hurt military man.[23]

The term "zoot suit" lived on throughout the war years, supposedly representing all boys who would not conform or do as expected, who carried a self-conscious, rebellious attitude. When two Brooklyn youths killed a teacher months after the Los Angeles summer trial of zoot-suiters, the *New York Times* headline shouted "Zoot Suit Youths Guilty." When the *Times* wrote of a new but inexperienced working-class audience for 1943 experimental theater productions in New York City, the paper chose to describe the rowdy young people as "Zoot-Suit Audiences." And in Portland, Oregon, the zoot-suit bias remained in hiring practices with employers stating that "trustworthy workers would not be the wearers of such queer raiment."[24]

Exaggerated clothing styles and rhyming slang continued throughout the war with such teenage phrases as "What's licking, chicken?" "What's fresh, presh?" "What's braggin, cousin?" "What's steamin', demon?" Clothing styles for young men, even in the Midwest, could be bright and distorted despite years of military influence. Rebellion remained. "The current style for daily wear as evinced by the boys of Des Moines," *Life* described, "consists of a loud flannel shirt, heavy white athletic socks and, if possible, wavy hair." They were given, like their sisters, to "extravagances of speech." Even a magazine such as *Successful Farmer* by the winter of 1946 poked fun at returning young military men who had perhaps become too used to conformity and khaki when they shunned the zoot suit.[25]

The zoot-suiter could never represent wartime unity with his defiant wastefulness. Perhaps he needed to experience a true combat zone, officials believed, to learn hard lessons about conformity of dress and military discipline as well as how to defend his country from outsiders, even to the death. But the "Zoot Suit Kids" in Los Angeles in the summers of 1942 and 1943 had been trying to do just that—defend their own home front from invaders.

In a 1943 poem that appeared in the *Saturday Evening Post,* both the urge to crush the nonconformist teenager yet a grudging respect for the consistent individuality existed in American wartime society.[26]

The Zoot-Suit Kid, he hung around
The Dutchman's place and danced and clowned,
While the hepcats laughed and the elders frowned—
The Kid with a fresh way, turning their hair gray,
  making the juke play,
All night long.

That Zoot-Suit Kid, the old folks said,
Was born in the alley and gutter-bred—
He'll die in a jail someplace, instead—
The Kid with a long coat, hair like a wild goat, ways
  like a young shoat
Wild and strong.

The Zoot-Suit Kid, he went to war,
Disposed of his pride on the day before,
Turned in his suit to a secondhand store—
Saying 'by to the hepcats, 'by to the street rats, 'by to
  the ersatz
Happy throng.

The Zoot-Suit Kid then dressed in brown
And he learned to watch for the sergeant's frown,
But the Army life didn't tone him down—
He was fresher than ever, would not endeavor not
  to be clever—
That was wrong.

No, the Zoot-Suit Kid they couldn't teach
Until that day they took the beach,
When the Zoot-Suit Kid he found his reach—
There on the sand dune, humming a swing tune, all the
  long forenoon,
Fighting well.

That Zoot-Suit Kid, he killed a lot,
With bayonet, hand grenade and shot,
Yes, he waded in where the fight was hot—
Finding his reach when, fearless, he fought then,
  bravest of brave men,
Till he fell.

Now the Zoot-Suit Kid he lies alone,
In a spot of earth that is all his own,
With just his name on a soldier's stone—
Dancing no more there, singing no jazz air, taking his
  last dare,
Lying long.

Yes, the Zoot-Suit hangs forlorn in the store,
But the tide brings a rhythm to that far-off shore,
And the Kid swings with it, though he doesn't know
the score—
Hep to the jive now, more than alive now, he shall
survive now,
In our song.

Although the term "zoot suit" lived on for a few more years after the war, the concept of juvenile delinquency would be challenged by young people themselves during the war years. A 1944 survey of more than six hundred boys and girls between fifteen and seventeen from schools across the country concluded that many young Americans felt "neither defensive nor defiant, and they were virtually unanimous in their indignation against the journalists' overemphasis on juvenile delinquency, remaining unimpressed with the grown-ups' standard solution—supervised recreation."

Rather, young people felt the better answer was to "attack the problem at the root." For many, that involved honestly addressing the easy availability of alcohol and the laxness of law enforcement in a wartime environment. "Many of the girls don't realize what they are doing," one New England girl answered, "because they are taken into bars and given drinks and most of them never had any liquor before. Then they get drunk and before they know it they are doing something they would not be likely to do otherwise." Another boy asked a series of difficult questions: "Why don't the police see to it that girls in bars aren't sold drinks? Why doesn't the Government enforce its law against selling young people liquor? Why don't the Army and Navy instruct sailors and soldiers to stop leading girls astray, to stop taking advantage of the silly, stupid ones who fall for their line and think it's glamorous to be a Victory girl?"

One seventeen-year-old New York girl voiced her concern, particularly about promiscuous sex, venereal disease, and pregnancy: "The rise in juvenile deliquency among girls has been particularly emphasized. That's not delinquency; that's really serious. But adults should stop and think before they call the majority of girls immoral." Or as another young girl concluded, "It's odd how grown-ups stress the wrong things. They're blind to the dangers of race discrimination, but they get terribly excited about the effects of boogie woogie."[27]

Emotions, moods, and hormones are difficult to control for adolescent girls and boys during the best of times, but this was particularly so during the war. In a romantic advertisement, the confident and caring American serviceman offers a Coke to a sweet and demure Irish girl. The setting might alter, but romance always seemed to be in the air. In reality, relationships between military men and local girls became much more fraught with complications, severely challenging traditional gender dimensions.[28]

Girls might resort to sneaking out without parental permission, but sometimes they were transported to military bases by the guardians themselves. With several thousand soldiers on furlough near San Antonio, Texas, busloads of "Liberty Belles" (girls supposedly seventeen- to twenty-five years old) along with a few chaperones traveled to the base for "carefully supervised visits." The Liberty Belles were instructed to be "sympathetic to troubles but careful with phone numbers." City officials even organized a contest for the prettiest of the Liberty Belles, but winner Agnes MacTaggert had to relinquish the questionable honor because she was only sixteen.[29]

Farther north along the rail line in Nebraska's North Platte, local townspeople organized a canteen to greet every troop train that passed through. "I wasn't old enough to work in the Canteen, even as a platform girl," apologized Doris Dotson, who was twelve at the war's beginning. Doris and her girlfriends would jitterbug to the jukebox, encouraging soldiers to join in and have some fun during their brief stop for the trains to refuel. "You know that expression, 'I'd rather dance than eat'?" Doris explained. "The boys would pass up the food tables to come down and dance with my friends and me." Although young Doris spent a lot of time dancing with military men at this small-town depot, her mother never seemed to worry about possible consequences to her well-being or her reputation. "As far as I was concerned," Doris concluded, "I was being very patriotic."[30]

While such behavior might be simply considered patriotic, the label quickly became "delinquent" when girls initiated the questionable contact. Across America, adults lamented the juvenile delinquency problem among teenage girls, and girls with perhaps tight sweaters and bright lipstick received such insulting labels as Liberty Belles, Victory Girls, uniform-chasers, khaki wackies, cuddle bunnies, round heels, patriotic amateurs, "patriotutes," chippies, or good-time Janes or Charlottes. As one war poster put it (blaming teenage girls rather than military men for any misbehavior and unintended consequences), "The Victory Girl Is Menace No. 1."[31]

This "distorted patriotism" meant that in Indianapolis girls of fifteen and sixteen frequented the bus depots to pick up servicemen when they reached town on leave. In Portland, girls twelve years old and up "clogged" Union Depot whenever a movement of troops occurred. In New York's Central Park, girls of fourteen or fifteen appeared so heavily made up that servicemen seemed confused regarding their "extreme youth." In Norfolk, police believed 85 to 90 percent of the prostitutes were "young amateurs." And in San Antonio, girls wearing hair ribbons, Sloppy Joe sweaters, and white anklets might perform "a strip-tease act whenever a uniform goes by."

War has always created unintended victims, but the media and adult authorities only criticized and rarely sympathized with these adolescent girls who were forced to grow up far too quickly because of changing wartime conditions and their own corresponding internal battles. Labeled promiscuous, the Victory Girls received the name-calling, blame, and possible consequences of an ever-present double standard.[32]

The United States also experienced its share of increased birthrates and sexually transmitted diseases due to wartime stresses and exhilarations. The birthrate dramatically increased in 1941 and 1942 and for years afterward as the average age of new mothers declined into the teen years. The maternity clothing industry began marketing to "junior mothers" as the defense boom brought on the baby boom. Each minute during 1941, more than four babies were born in the United States.[33]

Illegitimacy and baby black markets as well as illegal abortions also increased during the war years. The Children's Bureau acknowledged that fewer than half of the 48 states had laws to prosecute baby brokers, who now openly advertised with prices reaching $2,000 for an infant plus hospital expenses. Maud Morlock, a Children's Bureau consultant, confirmed it was common practice for unwed mothers to sign away their babies before or shortly after birth. Of the 3,259 adoptions recorded in Illinois, for example, only 885 were authorized by child welfare agencies or the Department of Public Welfare. In 1943, Chicago's illegitimate births rose to 20 percent.[34]

Still, the freedom of the times offered positive moments for American girls that they might not have otherwise experienced. "Some 6,000,000 U.S. teen-age girls live in a world all their own," *Life* wrote late in the war, "a lovely, gay, enthusiastic, funny and blissful society almost untouched by the war. It is a world of sweaters and skirts and bobby sox and loafers, of hair worn long, of eye-glass rims painted red with nail polish, of high-school boys not yet gone to war." For these "good girls," a tight sweater would be considered "the worst breach of etiquette," and "necking" at the movies remained "absolutely out."[35]

"When all the grown ups keep on telling kids how they shouldn't behave," a seventeen-year-old girl confessed, "it gets to be a dare." Teenagers responded to the charges of dramatically increased juvenile delinquency, and some young people offered their time and energy toward finding constructive solutions. In Port Jervis, New York, local boys and girls raised $130 from a scrap drive to start their own youth service, the Swing Inn, and adults commented favorably on "the community spirit" and "cooperative effort" demonstrated by the local teenagers in their fund-raising activities to build their project. "This is evidence that things can be done," the Port Jervis High School principal concluded, "and that the boys and girls will help." Teenagers in St. Paul, Minnesota, organized a youth center nicknamed the Teen Kanteen, and their adult coordinator commented that now their neighborhood "wouldn't have so many of the teenagers running around the streets at night."[36]

Speaking out for all teenagers in a patriotic fashion, a delinquency prevention agency of the New York Federation of Jewish Philanthropies composed a widely-circulated "Teen-Age Bill of Rights":

1. The Right to let childhood be forgotten
   (what is still cute to parents is embarrassing to teenagers)
2. The Right to a "say" about his own life
3. The Right to make mistakes, to find out for himself
4. The Right to have rules explained, not imposed
5. The Right to have fun and companions
6. The Right to question ideas
7. The Right to be at the romantic age
   (teenager love is serious—not "puppy love")
8. The Right to a fair chance and opportunity
9. The Right to struggle toward his own philosophy of life
10. The Right to professional help whenever necessary[37]

In March 1944, twelve teenagers visited President Roosevelt for the official signing of the May Day Child Health Day proclamation, and some of the president's young visitors offered their advice to counter the juvenile delinquency "problem." Joan Hickey, a seventeen-year-old from the crowded Texas boom town of Liberator Village, read her "Y" club telegram aloud: "We want security and a normal life after the war. We feel the high school educational program should fit us more adequately for the social and business world because most of us will not go to college." Hugh Willett, a sixteen-year-old from the textile mills of North Carolina, informed the president that boys now quit after the eighth grade to work in the mills where, as Hugh explained, "there are as many young people as there are older ones." Three teenagers—two black and one Chinese—raised "the question of racial prejudice." And Dolores Staven, a teenage member of North Dakota's Farmers Union, asked, "Couldn't the young folk have discussions and let the old people listen in?"

Finally at the Roosevelt youth discussion, Mary Rogers, a college student studying at Swarthmore who had both directed a survey of trailer towns and worked one summer with youth on the outskirts of Harlem, spoke up. Mary informed Roosevelt of her summer experience.

> This was a gang area. The gangs were organized along racial lines—a white gang, a Negro gang, and a Spanish gang. We opened a school as a project and started a newspaper, made posters, had dramatics, ran a salvage center. They were suspicious of us at first—thought we came in for uplift. It may not be a very polite thing to say in a place where there are so many social workers, but I think a lot of kids are tired of being taught morals with baseball.[38]

President Roosevelt must have nodded and tilted his head with his fatherly style in response to that youthful comment.

8

Gold Stars

Will my daddy be killed?

—"'Tell Children the Truth on War,' advises Dr. Andre Royon," *Washington Post* (March 25, 1942)

Ask the man who's coming home after the war to the youngster he's never seen. Does anything count except home?

—*Better Homes and Gardens* (June 11, 1945)

"I know you can't read this letter now," Captain Gerald Marnell began writing to his two-year-old daughter Geraldine, "but your mother will read it to you and she will save it for you until you are old enough to read it yourself." Marnell described his immense pride in a baby girl he barely knew: "Your daddy held you in his arms when you were only a few minutes old. Your daddy saw you grow. Then came a day when your daddy had to say good-bye. You cried so hard when daddy was driving away and daddy shed a tear himself. Your daddy didn't want to leave you, but he had to go to help make your country a safe and free place to live in." A devoted father, Marnell ended his letter with a promise that "he would be back someday to play together." This letter from Captain Marnell, age twenty-seven, would reach his wife two days before the telegram announcing his death.[1]

Marnell was not alone in his loneliness and his weariness. Near the end of 1944, another serviceman who was tired, miserable, hungry, and completely worn out told a war correspondent that "it's the kids who sharpen so many soldiers' thinking about Christmas." This "dirty doughfoot in

Paris" added, "I've got a wife and two kids back home sitting near a Christmas tree waiting for Santa Claus. They've been waiting three years."[2]

A year earlier on Christmas Eve, a little boy named Charlie de Turene from Seattle, Washington, decided to write to President Roosevelt after listening to his fireside chat. Charlie praised the president and commented about his own young life:

> I'm not so good at making speeches, but I want to say this—I am partly Russian and French and Belgium [*sic*], but I am most *"American"* and I'm proud of it. My uncle is in the Navy, and my cousin is a "Navy Pilot." I have got a $25.00 bond and 70 cents in stamps and I'm buying more. I mostly write to movie stars, but I think you as good as one. I go to a Catholic school and church. I am also Catholic. My Father is dead, but I do not wish to disscuss it. I have about a dime a day and from now on, instead of buying candy I am going to buy more stamps than ever. I hope you get time enough to read this small letter. I know how busy you are but I hope you get to read this.

A Steinway advertisement also captured this collective midwar sentiment, "Christmas . . . and the world at war. What do the uncertain years hold for your child?"[3]

The days and years of World War II deeply frightened most girls and boys in America—affecting them in profound and often silent ways. Adults expected children to remain "good little boys and girls" and to weather the storm of war and grief, but children had lots of imagination and many questions during the course of this war. Far too many questions remained unasked and therefore unanswered. Children possessed a number of fears as well, often unacknowledged or dismissed, and children shouldered their grief, sometimes by acting out but more often within a lingering silence. Carrying on as little soldiers appeared to be the only accepted response.

Wartime was never an optimal environment for raising healthy children; it complicated nearly everything: time, tension, tempers. The wish for peaceful times would be expressed in lines from Margaret Widdemeir's poem "For a Child in Wartime": "Let the world stay bright for her / She is little, she is young." The reality was much different. Even though American children were never in the midst of combat and occupation, the world at war seemed dark and frightening to young souls. Radio reports and newsreels continually brought home messages of danger and enemies, yet somehow hope usually remained for America's children. As ten-year-old Barbara June Caverlee of Virginia wrote to the president the day after Pearl Harbor, "I am hoping and praying for every boy in the Army and Navy and that they may come home alive."[4]

On D-Day (June 6, 1944), children poignantly presented their hopes, fears, and resiliency in letters to President Roosevelt. Davina Muir from Garden City, Michigan, listened to the president's prayer that day for a "Common Cause." "At ten o'clock this morning our bell at school rang for a minute of silence," Davina began writing. "In that moment I prayed and I shall continue to pray." Dwight Joll, a ten-year-old from South Fork, Pennsylvania, informed the president that he had heard "the nice prayer" on the radio and had tried to find a newspaper copy. "My daddy died last year but he was not in the army," Dwight explained. Nevertheless he still needed to pray on D-Day: "I have two cousins in the war one is a paratrooper and one is an aeral gunner."

Deciding to memorize the entire D-Day prayer by FDR, Sue Dakin from Warren, Ohio, surprised even her Sunday school teacher with her twelve-year-old determination. Little Florence Barnett not only prayed for the boys and our country but her president too. Although Florence called herself "a little nobody from Brooklyn," she believed the president when he said "my friends" on the radio. Leah Midgette from Atlantic City decided to send her D-Day letter across the ocean directly to General Eisenhower, praising her father who served in an invasion Coast Guard unit. General Eisenhower later wrote back to her, "You must be indeed proud of your father."[5]

D-Day was John Post's fourteenth birthday. "I remember coming down the stairs from my bedroom on that morning," John recalled, "and finding my father seated in his bathrobe, listening to the radio." Usually his father would be dressed and on his way to work but not that particular day. John forever remembered his father's exact words: "From now on, your birthday will be a famous day." D-Day was also Genny Kroepel's birthday, and this eleven-year-old found herself worrying more about the rain than what was going on overseas until her father came home. "Later that day, when my father returned home from work," recalled Genny, "we listened as usual to the war news on the radio. That's when I realized that this was a date I would have no trouble remembering in history class."[6]

When they had to say goodbye to the soldiers in their families, children became little adults. Parents expected children to "bid farewell" by shaking hands, shouldering responsibility, and blinking away tears because, at least in the beginning, wartime demanded dignity from every man, woman, and child. Fathers often felt torn between joining the military's war effort or staying with their family and community responsibilities. "I'm married and I've got a kid, but I had to get in this war," one recruit explained as he waved good-bye at the train station a few weeks after Pearl Harbor. Several life insurance companies created campaigns aimed at fathers who might long to leave for military service; the advertisement

Teenager Dale Dudgeon in front of the new family farm home in Brit, Iowa. His brothers served in the military. Courtesy of Joanne Dudgeon.

encouraged family men to remain on the home front, even without the possible rewards and glory of military service. As one ad admitted, "You don't get a medal for being a father."[7] But even in the midst of a terrifying world war, how could a father say good-bye to his children?

Even before Pearl Harbor, the U.S. military needed more men in anticipation of war. The initial draft in 1940, cleverly titled Bill 1776, met with some opposition, especially from women who did not want their sons involved in foreign wars; the Mothers' Crusade of 1940 designed and circulated formal cards—"Send this S.O.S.—Save Our Sons for Mother's Day"—in a gallant protest. But despite strong isolationist sentiments throughout the country, Congress enacted Bill 1776 (the Burke-Wadsworth Selective Service) on September 16, 1940. Initially, local draft boards preferred to draft single men, and as a result half a million more marriages than average were performed in late 1940 and early 1941 with a resulting increase in the birthrate in 1941 and 1942. By the end of 1942, conscription included eighteen- to twenty-year-olds rather than married men in proposed legislation nicknamed "the Teen Age Draft Bill."[8]

By October 1943, the military manpower situation had become even more desperate, and draft rules had to change again in order to meet necessary quotas. A 1943 Gallup poll found that 68 percent of Americans favored drafting single men before fathers even though the United States remained the only warring country to recognize "father status" and more than 80,000 fathers were already voluntarily serving in the military. Major

General Lewis Hershey, director of Selective Service, advised that by July 1944 the military would need 2 million more men in the European and Pacific theaters and a million of these draftees might be fathers.

When the Senate passed the Father Draft Act in October 1943 by a 69 to 0 vote, it eliminated the 3-A classification and exempt category for "pre-Pearl Harbor fathers" and doubled the military service child allotments, an increase in monthly pay based on family size. By July 1944, more than a million "pre-Pearl Harbor fathers" would be drafted. By the end of the war, almost one in five fathers between the ages of eighteen and thirty-seven was serving on active duty.[9]

Military conscription has always prompted social politics. Initially in 1940, some Americans objected to married men's exemptions, charging that they were "hiding behind women's skirts." Others believed that young men who did not maintain "a bona fide family relationship" should not be exempt, but child allotments for servicemen could prove costly, so government officials remained cautious about drafting family men. With allotments for his wife and eleven children, Private Arthur Christian from New York City was possibly the country's most expensive soldier as the Army was obligated to pay him $190 per month—a private's wages plus $140 for dependents.[10]

Sadly, the measure for Emergency Maternity and Infant Care would not pass Congress until May 1945. Although this bill provided medical care for wives and dependent children of the lowest four ranks of servicemen, some privileged congressional representatives argued that this medical care would be "charity." The legislation was finally passed by those in Congress who believed that "military husbands must be free from worry over their families."[11]

"Young Mr. 1942" was born to Lieutenant and Mrs. L. C. Holtzendorf at 12:00:35 in Atlanta, described not only enthusiastically as "a lusty son" but poignantly as "a war baby." In 1942, more babies were born in the United States than at any other time in history, and the birth rate continued to rise. More than 3 million babies were born in 1943, almost 45 percent more than in normal years. As *Time* magazine declared, "The wartime patter of little feet was being heard everywhere."[12]

But it was not always a bright start for America's infants. A number of babies were abandoned, some were adopted through black-market channels, and many children never saw their fathers, becoming war orphans. Ten-month-old Diane Morgan had never met her daddy, as he was a prisoner in Japan, but her mother held his photo up to her every day. And this little baby did have the modern opportunity to hear his voice on a recording. Her mother proudly claimed that little Diane had learned to recognize her father's image as she gurgled "Da-Da."[13]

Father absence lingered, but time nonetheless moved quickly for growing children. "You don't remember your father without a uniform . . ." began one piece of advertising copy, but Kellogg's joined in with yet another optimistic campaign about youth: "We need them strong!" adding that children would be facing "new and great responsibilities" in "the anxious years to follow." The federal government capitalized on children's complex wartime emotions when posters for the Fourth War Loan and succeeding bond campaigns used such guilt-inducing captions as "Please help bring my Daddy home."[14]

Parents wondered what to do to ease children's worries about wartime conditions. At the close of 1941, the Child Study Association of America published a fifteen-page booklet warning parents that children "take their cue from them in wartime." But as Sidonie Gruenberg, the leader of the association, recommended, families should not stoically offer either "grim silence" or "a pretense of courage" but rather "a frank and balanced recognition of a common danger." Gruenberg cautioned, "We have long known how foolish it is to try to deceive children."[15]

Other child experts offered similar advice. As the *Parents* author of "Facing War with Our Children" explained, "Our behavior in crises and normalcy is going to influence theirs." When boys and girls asked such questions as "Haven't they caught Hitler yet?" or "Will my daddy be killed?" these concerned children should receive answers and might gain great relief from "occasional direct and open talk about the war." Thus honesty became the consensus advice: "Whatever the age, children should not be lied to."[16]

Dealing directly with tragic news, however, has always been difficult. When five-year-old Jackie from Massachusetts received what proved to be the last letter from his father, his father requested that his little boy now "be a man."

> Dear Jackie,
>
> This is the first letter I have ever written directly to my little son, and I am thrilled to know you can read it by yourself. If you miss some of the words I am sure it will because I do not write plainly. Mother will help you in that case, I am sure.
>
> I was certainly glad to hear your voice over the long distance telephone. It sounded as though I were right there in the living room with you. You sounded as though you missed your daddy very much. I miss you, too, more than any one will ever know.
>
> It is too bad this war could not have been delayed a few more years so that I could grow up again with you and do all the things I planned to do when you were old enough to go to school.
>
> When you are a little bigger you will know why your daddy is not

> home so much anymore. . . . Unfortunately, there are some countries in the world where they don't have these ideals, where a boy cannot grow up to be what he wants to be, with no limits on his opportunities to be a great man, such as a great priest, statesman, doctor, soldier, business man, etc.
>
> If I don't get back, you will have to be mother's protector, because you will be the only one she has.

A few days after sending this letter to his young son, Jackie's father died in the sinking of the aircraft carrier *Wasp.*

Wanting to do something, sons and daughters felt helpless as they watched their grieving mothers cry out or silently give in. Published stories of families' concern did not always directly involve death, or, as one mother wrote, "It's the uncertainty of not knowing that wears you to a frazzle." It was her young son and daughter, however, who pulled her out of her depression, and this mother advised other parents not to carry all the strain but to try to make "partners of your children." Her daughter's determined outlook—to stop feeling sorry for her circumstances—pushed the mother out of her despondency. "Snap out of it, Mom," her daughter bravely admonished, "and we'll see what we can do."[17]

Fathers were not the only ones who left for war. Brothers, sisters, cousins, aunts, uncles, neighbors, and friends also faced military service, and with each loved one's leaving came worry, pain, fear, and guilt for the child left behind. When Danny Kelly of Pittsburgh, age twelve, looked at his family's service emblem in their window, it bore seven stars for his brothers. As director of the War Manpower Commission, Paul McNutt praised these children's stoic bravery in the face of such great possible loss, and he told high school boys and girls across the country that returning to school was their own military duty, and that they must meet the challenge "whole-heartedly" . . . "just as your older brothers are meeting their challenge all over the world."[18]

Sentiment and concern remained a two-way street during wartime. Overseas soldiers often wrote letters and sent packages with "souvenirs" from the battlefields to their little brothers and sisters at home, and although their words might be faint at times, their caring revealed itself. Samuel Aronson, a young man serving at the difficult Italian front, found time that summer of 1943 to write to his father about his younger brother. "Buddie's birthday is coming soon," Samuel noted. "Would you get him a little something for me—also a little remembrance to Granny?"[19]

In large and closely knit families, uncles and cousins were of direct concern for children. A nine-year-old boy from Anchorage, Alaska, wrote to President Roosevelt after a radio broadcast to offer his small but heartfelt

A girl with a military Christmas card. Courtesy of the State Historical Society of Iowa.

encouragement. "What I did understand of it made me even more sure we are going to beat the Axis. I have four uncles in the Navy that say we are too." Frank Santara Jr. wrote to President Roosevelt, praising his cousin at Pearl Harbor and suggesting a revised "teenage draft bill" so that fifteen-year-old boys like himself could serve. Frank thought that would be "grand" and concluded, "I am proud of my country."[20]

Even if one did not have extended family members who served, practically every American knew someone who did. Many teenagers who helped at the North Platte canteen in Nebraska thought daily of the soldiers' dangers as each troop train pulled through. "We were pretty much in awe of those soldiers and sailors, so close to our own ages," Floyd Burke later remembered. "I had a lot of respect for them, just looking at them in their uniforms."

"I remember thinking that I would have liked to go with them," reflected Eddie Yonker, who was thirteen at the time. "When you're a young boy, you want to be a part of all that. I knew they were going off to war, but I guess I didn't really understand what that meant." Another thirteen-year-old watched with mixed and wistful emotions. "You were delighted to greet the guys and give them home cooking," Helen Johnson recalled, "and as a teenager you liked to see the boys. But you also had this feeling in your heart that some would not make it home. You would look at them and feel a lump in your stomach thinking about their future. Seeing the young soldiers made me realize all the more that the war was a serious thing."

Marjorie Pinkerton, as a young teenager during the war years, not only saw "the boys" at the Nebraska canteen but imagined their struggles as she watched the newsreels in her small-town movie theater. "Without television back then, that is how we knew what the war looked like," Marjorie explained. "The battle coverage. It was black-and-white, and it would really bring it home. When you just heard about the war, you had to imagine things and picture it in your mind. But the newsreels made you see it."[21]

Sometimes family members' stories made the war seem very real. Ray Call, an eleven-year-old in Kansas, remembered conducting mock battles with the neighborhood kids. "We really had very accurate copies of weapons," Ray began, "and we were encouraged to play with them, because there was a great patriotic spirit and this was fostered in children." But when his uncle returned on military leave and began telling him some frightening stories, Ray recalled that it "began to sink in and I began to understand the horror of war." Seeing his uncle "reduced to a nervous basketcase" was "a terrible and vivid experience." "From that point on," Ray noted, "I began to understand war was hell."[22]

"War strain" was no single thing as psychologist Anna Wolf reminded her readers in *Our Children Face War*. Other child experts encouraged adult caregivers to remember that despite a confusing variety of war scenarios and emotions, children must be "safeguarded." The Children's Bureau's "Commission on Children in Wartime" issued a Children's Charter in Wartime with this concluding statement: "They must be nourished, sheltered, and protected even in the stress of war production so that they will be strong to carry forward a just and lasting peace." But as another child-care expert emphasized, no "calm fantasies" or "sugar-coated stories" would help children through their grief and guilt: "War is, of course, a tragic event, but on what grounds should we conclude that American children are to be spared the experience of tragedy? If tragedy exists in our world, will not the future be safer if children are aware of it? Children are braver than most adults assume."[23] The federal government, still capitalizing on children's images by the time of the Sixth War Loan, depicted two sad children peering through a window with a blue star above their heads. The poster's caption read, "For Father has been gone a long, long time."

"I am the happiest woman in the world," declared Hilda Bulkeley as she embraced her nineteen-month-old daughter, again showing the baby a picture of her father, a man she had never seen. The toddler looked skeptical as she gazed at the photograph, but "Daddy" was on his way home. What did that mean? Children were of course troubled when family men—as well as sisters and aunts—left for war, but children also worried about the return of their military fathers. How would life change again? Homecomings truly represented the end of war for America's children, much more so than official abstract markers like V-E and V-J Day. The formal signings of cease-fires and peace treaties would never be as important to a child as the initial sighting of a long-lost father, but the homecoming

Colonel Moore's homecoming to Villisca, Iowa. Courtesy of the *Omaha World-Herald.*

remained a complicated and not always happy event, fraught with emotions on all sides.

A Pulitzer Prize–winning photograph of a joyous return was that of Colonel Robert Moore as he stepped off the train at Villisca, Iowa. The small Midwestern town welcomed home their soldier from the North African front with many questions about their kin such as "How's my boy?" But it was the range of emotions in Moore's wife, daughter, and nephew that would be captured in that brief flashpoint. Seven-year-old Nancy was scooped up immediately by her father in a tight and loving embrace, her little legs dangling in the air. Moore's wife was understandably overwhelmed the moment she saw her husband, and her hands frantically framed her face. Standing to the side, a five-year-old nephew named Junior betrayed more skeptical but thoughtful emotions—and perhaps for that reason the little boy was cropped from the Pulitzer photo. The federal government later capitalized on this family photograph in a war-bond advertising campaign with the caption, "He'll be home a lot sooner if you buy more War Bonds now."[24]

A more somber homecoming photograph depicted amputee Private Isaac Pressley of Spartanburg, South Carolina. The private had been carried on stretchers, ambulances, hospital trains, and finally an Atlantic carrier to reach "his journey's end." When his wife and little girl and boy walked into the hospital ward, Private Pressley, as the newspaper reported, "really knew he was home at last." His long and difficult journey was over.[25]

More and more fathers would be returning home on stretchers, and *Newsweek* published a photograph in August 1945 of one military man lying on a hospital bed, holding his daughter's doll. That same week, when Private Elmer Robinson was lifted off a hospital plane at Hamilton Field, California, his wife and two younger daughters, ages four and five, greeted him after a year's absence. "Joanie," asked Private Robinson, "have you been a good girl?" The little girl kissed her daddy's cheek for the camera, replying, "Yes, Daddy, have you been a good boy?"[26]

"As much as the nation yearned for peace," writes the sociologist Suzanne Mettler in *The G.I. Bill and the Making of the Greatest Generation*, "its arrival brought new anxieties." The first concern was the most concrete: What would the homecoming be like?[27] It remained a dramatic story because of the classic elements of conflict, absence, love, safety, and home.

While those elements of the World War II homecoming have almost always been viewed and remembered through the eyes of the serviceman—his needs, wishes, desires, comforts, and fears—the child would necessarily possess a very different perspective. Calvin Christman of Texas remembers clearly, even though he was only three at the time, when his father came home in his "gray navy khaki uniform" and a newly acquired mustache. "Shaving that mustache was one of his first activities upon his arrival back home," Calvin remembers, "and I remembered quite clearly standing next to him, with my small hands tightly gripping the washstand, looking up at this wonderful man as he shaved. To this day, it remains my most precious early memory."[28]

After several years of war, children were noticeably older but so too was Father. He had been one of 16 million servicemen, and whether he had seen combat or not, he had certainly changed. He had been through military training and wartime experience, becoming accustomed to discipline, order, regimentation, and hierarchy. His world had consisted of loud voices from above and constant grumbling from below. He had learned strong concepts of power and leadership, and he had perhaps lived through horrific scenes of life-threatening chaos. The military had made strange demands on his emotions, sometimes taxing him to his personal limits. This combination of strict military training and possible trauma for the father would not always fit easily into a household with children who needed firmness, discipline, and rules but also flexibility, reassurance, warm touches, caring voices, and loving feelings. Fathers and their children often felt like complete strangers to each other—unsure of how to act, touch, and cope. Still, as *Parents* magazine promised, the homecoming could be positive, if patience and understanding were present.[29]

Life without Father had probably been difficult with the children's anger often directed initially toward the present parent, the mother. Somewhat comfortable routines soon developed although father substitutes and masculine patterns were probably difficult to find. Over the war-torn years father had been calmly represented by a service star in the window, a portrait on the mantel, and letters in the mailbox. What would reality be like for the children upon his return?[30]

A week after V-E Day, eleven-year-old Philip Brown of San Francisco wrote for his English class the winning essay titled "The First Day My Father Is Home." Although Philip's composition technically fit the prescribed five-paragraph structure, the final two "paragraphs" indicated that the young author was quite uncertain of what might happen after the initial homecoming.

> My father has been out in the Pacific for about 15 months. In three months he is due home. I wonder what the first day home will be like. This is how I think it will be.
>
> Mom, Steve, Jim, and myself will all go down to meet him at the pier. The ship will be late. Many people will be waiting. When it arrives we shall find my father. I would start asking so many questions.

> Pop would not answer all of them. He would want to forget the war now that he was home. By the time we got home it would be lunch time. He would then eat his first home cook meal in one and a half years. I am sure we shall have a very fancy lunch. After about an hour eating, filling quite full, mom will ask me to get the schoch out and start on drinks. (Oh Boy.) At about three, pop will want some good old modern music. Then a few friends will come in to welcome him home with a bottle of sckoch. After awhile we shall start getting hungry. (Food!)
>
> Mom says, "Let's go out to dinner and be stylish about it."
>
> After food, bed! Oh Boy.

A psychologist named George Robert Bach at Western Reserve University used "a role-play technique" to determine young children's feelings about their absent father and his return from the war. In his research, Bach found that the absent military father had become "a veritable paragon," a fantasy in which he does what the child pleases, such as throwing parties, buying ice cream, and displaying constant affection. Bach offered this seven-year-old girl's fantasy as representative of the children he studied:

> Father says, "Let's go to the picture show." Little girl and little boy dance round and round, then they all go to the picture show. After awhile they come back and Father goes down in the cellar to fix the pipes 'cause Mother told him there was a leak in the water pipe. Then he comes upstairs and washes the dishes and Mother dries them and then he kisses Mother and hugs her and then he kisses the little girl and little boy and says, "You better go on to bed now." But they say, "Oh, can't we stay up and play awhile?" And Father says, "All right."[31]

Many soldiers found that once they were home it was difficult to adjust to the constant noise, interruptions, and decisions required in domestic life. Richard Werner confessed that as a young father he "wrestled with considerable anxiety." Werner certainly was not alone. Yet most men remained silent about their fears and depression. Serving with the 442d Regimental Combat Team of Japanese American men and wounded by a sniper's bullet that had creased his skull, Mickey Akiyama returned to a home he had never seen before because his wife had been interned during the war years, and he greeted a baby daughter born shortly after he left for service in his segregated unit. The little girl, of course, did not recognize her father, and he suffered not only from his long military absence but from headaches, dizziness, and other symptoms of his injury for decades to come. The scars and wounds of World War II, both inside and out, often took years if not decades to heal or at least fade.[32]

Sometimes children were dramatically called upon to receive their fathers' posthumous medals. General George C. Marshall personally pinned the medal on young Robert Stevens, who received his father's Distinguished Service Cross, and six-year-old Nancy Jane Clayton accepted her father's Congressional Medal of Honor in a room filled with admirals and senators. When Secretary of War Henry Stimson pinned her father's Purple Heart and Silver Star on six-week-old Ann Hamilton Landess, the baby became an official member of the "Cradle Roll of Honor."

During the course of the Second World War, 405,399 American men died and 607,846 were injured. Only the Civil War had a higher death toll. An estimated 183,000 home front children lost their fathers during World War II. As a veteran and historian of this war who remains unafraid of grappling with difficult truths, Paul Fussel writes in *The Day the War Ended*, "It's the living who are the casualties."[33]

In the late afternoon of April 6, 1945, in the last days of the European war, a four-year-old boy would forever remember how his mother was making supper when her two female friends came to call, delivering the bad news. "Clyde was called home," one of her friends hesitantly began. "He was called to his heavenly home." This little boy could not understand why his mother continued to cry, and she didn't explain anything to him until he called her into the bathroom and asked her why she kept sobbing. During these painful moments inside their house, his father's best friend, who worked as a messenger for the post office, could not bring himself to deliver the fateful telegram. This kind man who could not bear to see a woman's tears waited outside the house in his car and cried.[34]

Also near the end of the war, John Nichols Jr., age nine, remembered playing on the streets of his upstate New York hometown one day when "the news" arrived. His mother came home from work that night and received the telegram. "She just went out of it," John remembered. "It seemed like that's all she did was lie on the couch and cry."

That boy and the 183,000 other war orphans have carried emotional scars for the rest of their lives. Even fifty years later, their wartime reflections are weighted with haunting words:

Vince: "There is a part of me down deep which never heals . . ."

Eric: "I don't think you ever get over it . . ."

Connie: "I remember the cake . . . the package that came back . . ."

Clatie and John: "We don't know how he died . . ."

John: "When I had my own children, I didn't know what to do . . ."

Mary: "You're out there on your own . . ."

Jeff: "I expect people to die on me all the time . . ."

Sheila: "My father probably never knew that I had been born . . ."[35]

"Daddy, President Roosevelt is dead," ten-year-old Emilie informed her father. "No," he said. "Impossible. That must be a mistake." "No, no, I heard it over the radio," she assured him. Frank Hubert felt compelled to share his story of grief, as would thousands of other Americans, to First Lady Eleanor Roosevelt on April 12, 1945.

Many of these condolence letters and cards were spontaneously sent by children. "He has been president ever since I can remember," wrote Marian Whitaker from Pocatello, Idaho, to the First Lady. "It just doesn't seem true to me yet. All the pupils, teachers, and the principal at my school looked like they could burst into tears at any moment." For America's younger children, Franklin Delano Roosevelt had been the only president they had ever known. As Barbara Anar from Tulsa, Oklahoma, said in a note to the First Lady, "I am writing this letter to tell you I am sorry that President Roosevelt had to leave this earth right when we need him most and hope we can get along without him, but I don't think we can." As an elementary schoolgirl named Helen Frances Shugars concluded, "I am very sorry to hear of President Roosevelt's death. I liked President Roosevelt very much and I admired his courage. I felt sure of winning the war when he was President." Another little girl, Barbara Ellen Floyd, poignantly scrawled, "I was counting very much on him to bring home my father."

So many children (and adults) simply "didn't believe it" when they first heard the news, and then they cried from shock and true grief. President Roosevelt had been their war leader. He had helped children with infantile paralysis. Children had donated their money to war bonds as if to him directly. And now he was gone. "So to me he was the first President in my life," wrote young Audriana Ntiros, "and it will be hard to get used of hearing someone else as President instead of Franklin Delano Roosevelt." Bennie James Powell of Detroit composed the following: "I am a boy of ten. I thought I would write a verse to tell what I think of a Great man."

> We love Mr. Roosevelt. We will miss him.
> He helped us when we were at war
> and did not live to see the end.
> He planned it well
> and did not see it all work.
> He was a good man and a good leader.

On May 7, 1945, twenty-four children (all members of the Junior Red Cross) from Humbercrest Elementary School in California performed a "United Nations" play. Although these children had always known war because they were born in the late 1930s, the emerging new world with its emphasis on the "United Nations" concept brought the children a peaceful postwar promise of hope. Wrote Timothy, "And I'm glad he was our President. I am glad V.E. day has come. And I'm glad peace has nearly come." Or as Carol Coles believed, "Now that V.E. day has come and peace is in the air, I hope that we will be—just and righteous—as Roosevelt would wish as he stood for goodwill. We sang the Russian song United Nations."[36]

From this same elementary school, eight-year-old David Bushey's perspective in May 1945 beautifully captured the childlike ending of World War II with its drama and its sorrow, its grief and its confusion, its hope and its promise:

> Dear Mrs. Roosevelt:
> We put a play the play was united Nations and how sorry we were to lose him. He was my best friend and stallen is a good friend and Im realy sorry that Mr roosevelt is Dead and I am 8 years old now VE day has come and it isent isn't exactly over and on VE day I had a good time and I hope you had a good time to.

The Second World War for America's children was almost over but never to be forgotten.

Conclusion

The Forgotten Generation

War was always worse than I knew how to say—always.

—Martha Gellhorn, U.S. war correspondent, *Monte Cassino: The Hardest-Fought Battle of World War II* (2004)

Perhaps the most common myth about war is that it ends when the textbooks say it does, when the cease-fires begin and the documents are signed.

—Ann Hagedorn, *Savage Peace: Hope and Fear in America 1919* (2007)

"Dad, Dad," clamored some children trying to rouse their father at three in the morning. "Will our big brother be coming home?" "Sure, sure," he muttered, "just go back to sleep. . . ." This anonymous family reflected the hopes and anxieties of so many thousands. As the eager children knew before the adults could comprehend, the war was over.[1]

At three that afternoon, a crowd of 75,000 men, women, and children gathered in Lafayette Park across from the White House, chanting, "Harry, Harry. We want Harry!" Conga lines of soldiers, sailors, women, teenagers, and children began dancing around the park's lawn. Now the "benign" sun shone on America rather than the rising sun of Japan. President Truman appeared before the crowd. "Ladies and gentlemen," he began his formal announcement, "this is a great day. This is the day we have all been looking for since December 7, 1941. This is the day when fascism and police government ceases in the world." Half an hour later the president of the United States called his ninety-three-year-old mother to tell her the good news. His mother later said to reporters, "I'm glad Harry decided to end the war."

A "conga line" in front of the White House on V-J Day. Courtesy of the FDR Library and Archives.

After the phone call, the president could not resist the "mad joy" of the people, later joining them in Lafayette Park. Young and old alike tried to push their heads through the White House fence—screaming, laughing, crying with joy. Reluctant police with bayonets could not control the crowds. "Washington had never seen this kind of celebration," one reporter claimed as the final words from the White House rang out: "It's all over."

Moments after the announcement in New York's Chinatown, four dragons—traditional symbols of peace, prosperity, and health—began snaking through the streets flanked by a man hammering a Chinese gong and two boys clanging cymbals. This "Victory Joy" noise accompanied hundreds of firecrackers popping and automobile horns honking. A trampled, paper-filled effigy of the Japanese emperor also became part of the parade. At exactly 7:03 p.m. in New York City's Times Square, the electric sign flashed with three stars, symbolizing peace. The crowd grew to more than half a million people that celebratory day. In Brooklyn's Italian American neighborhoods, tables loaded with food, wine, and liquor quickly lined the streets. In Harlem, the "uproarious" celebration filled the streets with couples "jiving" until a sprinkler truck sprayed the crowds to clear a route for standstill traffic. In St. Patrick's Cathedral, thousands of residents arrived during the evening for prayers of thanksgiving. In Boston's joyous gathering, a baby dressed in a tiny sailor suit would be raised above the crowd as a victory symbol. In San Francisco, crowds of men, women, and children thronged Market Street all day long. Everywhere in America, the celebrating seemed to have no end, with "a mad bedlam" of blowing bugles, beating washtubs, banging pans, blasting horns, bellowing sirens, and clanging bells. Everywhere people kept waving flags, throwing paper, and chugging beer. As *Newsweek* described the frenzy of fun from Washington, D.C., to Miami to Kansas City to Los Angeles, "The Men of War Kiss from Coast to Coast." Or as a Southern reporter summed up the day's passionate celebrating, "Sailors kissed girls, and girls kissed sailors."[2]

Particularly at their ends, wars have always been measured not only in wondrous concluding-moment emotions but in numbers. In seventeen days, less than a full six years from the Nazis' September 1, 1939, invasion of Poland, World War II had cost the world over 55 million deaths and a trillion dollars. The United States alone endured over a million casualties and spent $300 billion in its three years, eight months, and seven days of direct participation in this world war. Japanese citizens would consider V-J Day the darkest day in their two-thousand-year history, but as the *Atlanta Constitution* surmised, "It—the war, the costliest war in blood, dollars, and resources in history—was over."[3]

This book is only a beginning. Of the approximately 450 books written about the United States during the Second World War in a major U.S. research university library, only five are concerned specifically with American children. This book adds to a late beginning telling the story of more than 30 million young people in America between birth and sixteen years old who lived and worked through three and a half years of the most traumatic period in world history.

Sadly, America's children of that war have become a forgotten generation. Historically they have been squeezed between the "Greatest Generation," those old enough to actively serve in the struggle against the Axis, and the "Baby Boomers," a generation too young to have memories of the war. These two well-known demographic groups, because of their sheer numbers and their recognized role in history, have overshadowed the unending work and countless sacrifices of the generation of children born between the two, children who grew up all too quickly and became young soldier citizens during the years of World War II.

Richard and Kathleen [Hurley] Payne holding hands in front of their home near Ottumwa, Iowa, 1945. Courtesy of Richard Payne.

Richard and Kathleen [Hurley] Payne on their Navy brother's Indian Chief motorcycle, after the war. Courtesy of Richard Payne.

The forgotten generation experienced the flashpoint of that Pearl Harbor Sunday, and their childhood experiences became locked in fear and fascination for what this strange event would portend. As children, they would forever remember not only the day's events but also their parents' faces and actions. What was war? What would happen to their families and their country? What were they to do? As the historian Stephen Ambrose once declared, "Pearl Harbor burned itself into the souls of a generation."[4]

This was the generation called upon to enter schools that were crowded and unprepared for them with shortages of teachers and basic resources such as books and food. They studied a confusing curriculum geared to war. Yet this generation contributed more than two billion dollars in nickels and dimes brought to school each week for their nation's war bonds in response to constant demands for support.

This generation organized and motivated themselves, their families, and their neighbors to gather and sort—with no real reward or compensation—the salvaged materials needed to fight an industrial war as well as to cultivate victory gardens for the food at their school lunches or family dinners, allowing increased shipments to the American military and allied countries. This generation knew the importance of "clean plates" because, as they were constantly reminded by their elders, other children around the world were starving. And this generation understood the global importance of recycling efforts and growing local food long before this current generation. Unfortunately, without the "red" motivation of war, the "green" movement could not be sustained.

This young generation tried to play despite shortages of manufactured toys by creating interesting and aggressive games of war in infinite variations to act out their personal stresses in a violent world. Despite concerned adults' attempts to limit children's playtime, boys and girls found many ways to pretend and create. Play helped this generation express hope and fear, cope with confusion and pain, inspire curiosity and courage, and release anger and energy.

This generation went to work—paid and unpaid—in housework, service jobs, factory positions, and agricultural labor—and sometimes gave up the chance to earn a high school degree as they contributed to their country's war effort. Parents, teachers, and government officials expected and sometimes demanded war work from children, but this generation of soldier citizens rarely complained.

This generation left behind family and friends, schools and neighborhoods to travel to unwelcoming communities unprepared for children's basic needs of housing and schooling. Many Japanese Americans in this generation were forced to live three years of their childhood behind barbed wire. Other minority children endured discrimination, violence, and segregation within these new communities even during an era of "united nations."

Some children of this generation were too quickly labeled juvenile delinquents for succumbing to the tension and excitement of the wartime world of risk and danger. Their anxious and overwhelmed parents could not always take care of everything that needed to be done, and children noisily acted out or suffered silently.

This generation endured absences of their fathers, brothers, sisters, cousins, aunts, uncles, neighbors, and friends sent to the machine of war. They saw the blue and gold stars in their windows, wondered about the long absence of their father and the "strange man" who reappeared in their living rooms or perhaps, sadly, grieved forever over the death of a father. Thousands of war orphans never forgot the pain or recovered their childhood.

Among this generation were happy scrappers and diligent victory gardeners with a strong sense of community, but they were also the children who worked long hours for little reward and who were often left alone and afraid—young soldier citizens and small waifs of war. They were a generation too often brave beyond their years.

This is the generation that should not be forgotten.

Notes

Introduction: A Child's Perspective on World War II

1. Jordan Braverman, *To Hasten the Homecoming: How Americans Fought World War II through the Media,* 226; and Marc Scott Miller, *The Irony of Victory: World War II and Lowell, Massachusetts,* 187.
2. Stephen E. Ambrose, *Americans at War,* vii.
3. William M. Tuttle Jr., *"Daddy's Gone to War": The Second World War in the Lives of America's Children,* 45.

Chapter 1: Almost Christmastime

1. Ethelyn Myhre, *Hawaiian Yesterdays,* no page numbers; *Time,* December 15, 1941, 19; George Sullivan, *The Day Pearl Harbor Was Bombed: A Photo History of World War II,* 5; Margaret Chase Smith Library, "Washington and You," vol. 2, January 21, 1943; and Gordon Prange with Donald M. Goldstein and Katherine V. Dillon, *December 7th, 1941: The Day the Japanese Attacked Pearl Harbor,* 107. *Kaminas* translated (in 1942) to "long-settled whites."
2. Terry Dunnahoo, *Pearl Harbor: America Enters the War,* 20, 21, 57, 78, and 93; Thomas B. Allen, *Pearl Harbor: American and Japanese Survivors Tell Their Stories,* 16; and Prange, *December 7th,* 115.
3. Prange, *December 7th,* 22, 23, 120, 121, 164, 175, and 196; Robert S. LaForte and Ronald E. Marcello, editors, *Remembering Pearl Harbor: Eyewitness Accounts by U.S. Military Men and Women,* 252; and Dorinda Makanaonalani, *Pearl Harbor Child: A Child's View of Pearl Harbor from Attack to Peace,* 15.
4. Prange, *December 7th,* 212.
5. *New York Review of Books,* March 15, 1942, 8; Prange, *December 7th,* 22 and 23; and Max Boot, *War Made New: Technology, Warfare, and the Course of History, 1500 to Today,* 242.
6. Prange, *December 7th,* 120.
7. Prange, *December 7th,* 121.
8. Prange, *December 7th,* 164.
9. Gordon Prange with Donald M. Goldstein and Katherine V. Dillon, *At Dawn We Slept: The Untold Story of Pearl Harbor,* 567.
10. LaForte and Marcello, *Remembering Pearl Harbor,* 253.
11. Prange, *December 7th,* 175.

12. Prange, *December 7th,* 196.
13. Makanaonalani, *Pearl Harbor Child,* 16.
14. Prange, *December 7th,* 196.
15. Prange, *December 7th,* 168; and *Portland Press Herald,* December 7, 1991, 10A.
16. LaForte and Marcello, *Remembering Pearl Harbor,* 202; and Allen, *Pearl Harbor,* 45.
17. Wallace B. Black and Jean F. Blashfield, *Pearl Harbor!* 27 and 28; and LaForte and Marcello, *Remembering Pearl Harbor,* 116 and 124.
18. LaForte and Marcello, *Remembering Pearl Harbor,* 148.
19. *Time,* December 15, 1941, 22; and Prange, *At Dawn We Slept,* 520.
20. Blake Clark, *Remember Pearl Harbor!* 17, 18, 34, 35, 61, 62, and 218.
21. La Forte and Marcello, *Remembering Pearl Harbor,* 30.
22. K. D. Richardson, *Reflections of Pearl Harbor: An Oral History of December 7, 1941,* 47.
23. Prange, *At Dawn We Slept,* 566.
24. Dunnahoo, *Pearl Harbor,* 35.
25. *Washington Post,* March 8, 1942, 10; and Makanaonalani, *Pearl Harbor Child,* 18.
26. *Des Moines Tribune,* January 6, 1942, 1; *Des Moines Register,* December 18, 1941, 1; Prange, *December 7th,* 230 and 351; Carl Smith, *Pearl Harbor: The Day of Infamy,* 74; and Blake, *Remember Pearl Harbor!* 82 and 83.
27. Richardson, *Reflections of Pearl Harbor,* 144; and "Memories from the Homefront: A Date which Will Live in Infamy," *Michigan History Magazine* (November/December 1991): 36.
28. Richardson, *Reflections of Pearl Harbor,* 62, 63, and 158.
29. Richardson, *Reflections of Pearl Harbor,* 78 and 79.
30. Robert Kirk, *Earning Their Stripes: The Mobilization of American Children in the Second World War,* 16; "Memories from the Homefront," 34; and Richardson, *Reflections of Pearl Harbor,* 85.
31. "Memories from the Homefront," 34.
32. Studs Terkel, *"The Good War": An Oral History of World War II,* 8; and Richardson, *Reflections of Pearl Harbor,* 80.
33. Richardson, *Reflections of Pearl Harbor,* 76; and "Memories from the Homefront," 38.
34. Richardson, *Reflections of Pearl Harbor,* 44 and 45.
35. Prange, *December 7th,* 358; LaForte and Marcello, *Remembering Pearl Harbor,* 202; and *Des Moines Tribune,* December 29, 1941, 16. Numbers vary in different accounts. Americans suffered over 2,000 military deaths, and approximately 50 to 70 civilians died near Pearl Harbor, Honolulu, and Wahiawa. The Japanese lost 185 pilots through death and one as prisoner. Smith, *Pearl Harbor,* 75; John Toland, *Infamy: Pearl Harbor and Its Aftermath;* and *Time,* December 15, 1941, 22.
36. Sullivan, *The Day Pearl Harbor Was Bombed,* 10.
37. Franklin D. Roosevelt Presidential Library, PPF 200B, Public Reaction, file: December 8, 1941 [John Barry School].
38. Franklin D. Roosevelt Presidential Library, OF 4675, World War II, box 6: Support A-B.

39. Toland, *Infamy,* 31; Makanaonalani, *Pearl Harbor Child,* 35; *Honolulu Star Tribune,* March 13, 1942, 1; and *New York Times,* February 28, 1942, 11.

40. *New York Times,* February 26, 1942, 18; Margaret Chase Smith Library, "Washington and You," speech titled "Hawaii," July 2, 1945; Margaret Chase Smith Library, scrapbook #25, Investigation of Congested Areas: A Report on the Pearl Harbor-Honolulu Area; *Life,* May 11, 1942, 90; and *New York Times,* February 28, 1942, 11. The civilian population on Oahu increased from 229,856 in 1940 to 337,535 on December 31, 1944—a 47 percent increase from 107,679.

41. *New York Times,* December 10, 1941, 1.

42. *Atlanta Constitution,* January 1, 1942, 2; *Des Moines Register,* January 1, 1942, 1; *New York Times,* December 26, 1941, 1; LaForte and Marcello, *Remembering Pearl Harbor,* 258; *New York Times,* January 1, 1942, 7; and *Washington Post,* March 8, 1942, 1.

43. *Des Moines Register,* January 1, 1942, 8.

44. *Des Moines Tribune,* December 22, 1941, 3; and *New York Times,* November 25, 1941, 32.

45. *Atlanta Constitution,* December 15, 1941, 2; *Washington Post,* December 4, 1941, 14; *Atlanta Constitution,* December 18, 1941, 14; and *Des Moines Register,* December 18, 1941, 9.

46. David Stafford, *Roosevelt and Churchill: Men of Secrets,* 125; and *New York Times,* December 25, 1941, 13.

47. Kenneth Davis, *Franklin D. Roosevelt: The War President, 1940–1943,* 368.

48. *Atlanta Constitution,* January 13, 1942, 1.

49. Elizabeth Mullener, *War Stories: Remembering World War II,* 32 and 33.

Chapter 2: Schools for War

1. *New York Times,* December 8, 1941, 1.

2. Richardson, *Reflections of Pearl Harbor,* 83; David E. Hanson, "Home-Front Casualties of War Mobilization: Portland Public Schools, 1941–1945," *Oregon Historical Quarterly* 96, no. 2–3 (Summer–Fall 1995): 194.

3. *Des Moines Tribune,* December 8, 1941, 1; and Richardson, *Reflections of Pearl Harbor,* 75.

4. Kirk, *Earning Their Stripes,* 16; and *Des Moines Tribune,* December 12, 1941, 11.

5. *New York Times,* February 15, 1942, 13.

6. *New York Times Magazine,* February 22, 1942, 12.

7. *Washington Post,* December 11, 1941, 25; and *Education for Victory,* June 1, 1942, 1.

8. *Des Moines Tribune,* December 12, 1941, 11.

9. *Des Moines Tribune,* December 19, 1941, 26; and December 20, 1941, last page; and *New York Times,* February 18, 1942, 16; and May 12, 1942, 3.

10. *Washington Post,* December 11, 1941, 18.

11. *New York Times,* December 11, 1941, 20; and December 10, 1941, 16.

12. *Washington Post,* December 24, 1941, 19.

13. New York State Archives, Citizen Unity Projects, A4270–78, box 2 of 2, folder Schools at War; and *Education for Victory,* October 15, 1942, 7.

14. Tuttle, *"Daddy's Gone to War,"* 115.

15. *Education for Victory,* March 1, 1943, 6; Kirk, *Earning Their Stripes,* 86; *Education for Victory,* March 15, 1943, 30; *Washington Post,* March 25, 1942, 15; *Education for Victory,* July 15, 1942, 42; and *Parents,* January 1943, 15 and 32.

16. *Education for Victory,* December 15, 1942, 11; and *Education for Victory,* July 15, 1942, 1.

17. *Los Angeles Times,* April 8, 1942, 1; and *New York Times,* May 15, 1942, 9.

18. Anna W. M. Wolf, *Our Children Face War,* 70; Patricia Albjerg Graham, *Schooling America: How the Public Schools Meet the Nation's Changing Needs,* 1, 3, and 5.

19. American Jewish Archives, Frank Weil Papers (box 14, folder 14/6), letter dated September 15, 1942.

20. *World Over,* March 17, 1944, 2; and *New York Times,* May 15, 1942, 9.

21. New York State Archives, Citizen Unity Projects, A4270–78, box 1 of 2, folder Albany—Education Committee of Albany—Defense Council: The Report of the Initial Meeting of the Advisory Council on Education for the Office of Civilian Mobilization, led by Chard Bates, chairman of the Albany Student War Council; and *New York Times,* October 4, 1942, 5.

22. New York State Archives, Citizen Unity Projects, A4270–78, box 1 of 2, folder Albany—Education Committee of Albany folder, letter dated December 4, 1942, as well as folder: Albany—Education Committee of Albany: Bibliography of Economic and Social Study Material; and *Atlanta Constitution,* February 20, 1942, 4.

23. *Successful Farming,* July 1944, 52.

24. *New York Times,* January 10, 1942, 7; and *Los Angeles Times,* October 17, 1942, 1/Society.

25. *New York Times,* January 14, 1942, 11; John S. Westerlund, "Bombs from Bellemont: Navajo Ordnance Depot in World War II," *Journal of Arizona History* 42, no. 3 (Autumn 2001): 335.

26. *New York Times,* December 16, 1941, 22.

27. *Education for Victory,* May 3, 1945, 7; and Kirk, *Earning Their Stripes,* 96.

28. *New York Times,* April 26, 1942, 15; and *Iowa PTA,* June-July 1945, 1. American Victory clubs numbered 88,000 members in 5,000 schools nationwide.

29. *New York Times,* June 10, 1942, 14.

30. *New York Times,* July 12, 1942, 16.

31. *Education for Victory,* July 1, 1942, 3; and *World Over,* May 19, 1944, 19.

32. *Atlanta Constitution,* February 1, 1942, 6C.

33. *New York Times,* August 15, 1943, 10X; *Time,* June 21, 1943, 48; and American Heritage Center, University of Wyoming Archives, Wyoming Retired Teachers' Association Collection, accession number 6467: Ruth Linder.

34. *New York Times,* December 14, 1942, 15; and *New York Times,* December 20, 1942, E7.

35. *Newsweek,* September 28, 1942, 60; and Richard J. Evans, *The Third Reich in Power, 1933–1939,* 265.

36. *Life,* February 1, 1943, 37 and 40; *Newsweek,* February 1, 1943, 70; and *Time,* January 18, 1943, 43.

37. *Time,* June 25, 1945, 59.

38. *New York Times,* November 23, 1941, 6D; *Parents,* October 1943, 17; and Patrick G. O'Brien, "Kansas at War: The Home Front, 1941–1945," *Kansas History* 17, no. 1 (Spring 1994): 9.

39. *Time,* September 4, 1943, 42; *New York Times,* October 17, 1943, E7; and *Newsweek,* August 30, 1943, 98.

40. Graham, *Schooling America,* 31 and 106; *New York Times,* September 12, 1943, 11; and March 14, 1943, E9; *Education for Victory,* September 1, 1942, 1; and *Time,* April 27, 1942, 44.

41. *Education for Victory,* January 20, 1944, 1; and July 20, 1944, 6; *Parents,* October 1943, 17; and *Time,* September 4, 1943, 42.

42. American Heritage Center, University of Wyoming Archives, Wyoming Retired Teachers' Association Collection, accession number 6467.

43. *New York Times,* September 14, 1943, 25.

44. *Education for Victory,* December 15, 1943, 13.

45. "Editorial: The War and After," *Understanding the Child* 12, no. 2 (June 1943): 17; and Joseph M. Hawes, *Children between the Wars: American Childhood, 1920–1940,* 11.

46. *Time,* September 11, 1944, 72.

47. *Wallaces' Farmer,* April 3, 1943, 5.

48. *Time,* December 4, 1939, 54; *New York Times,* October 5, 1944, 14; and Ann Short Chirhart, *Torches of Light: Georgia Teachers and the Coming of the Modern South,* 155–56.

49. *New York Times,* April 29, 1943, 24; Paul G. Merriam, Thomas J. Molloy, and Theodore W. Sylvester Jr., *Home Front on Penobscot Bay: Rockland during the War Years, 1940–1945,* 129; and *New York Times,* February 21, 1943, 15X.

50. *Saturday Evening Post,* July 4, 1942, 28.

51. *Wallaces' Farmer,* September 18, 1943, 26; and *Successful Farming,* January 1942, 47.

52. Margaret Chase Smith Library, Washington and You, May 11, 1944; and Statements and Speeches, 79th Congress, 1945–1946, vol. 3, March 22, 1945.

53. American Jewish Archives, Alice B. Citron (small collections), letter with no date.

54. Martin Gilbert, *The Day the War Ended: May 8, 1945—Victory in Europe,* 297.

Chapter 3: Kid Salvage

1. *Life,* January 11, 1943, 16 and 17.

2. *Atlanta Constitution,* January 11, 1942, 8.

3. *New York Times,* November 12, 1941, 28.

4. Bruce C. Smith, *The War Comes to Plum Street,* 115.

5. *Parents,* July 1942, 21; and Hanson, "Home-Front Casualties," 192.

6. Kirk, *Earning Their Stripes,* 74; and Hanson, "Home-Front Casualties," 202.
7. Kirk, *Earning Their Stripes,* 56, 64, and 65; and *New York Times,* September 20, 1942, 33.
8. *New York Times,* January 21, 1942, 15; and April 23, 1943, 14; *Time,* June 15, 1942, 14; and *Saturday Evening Post,* December 12, 1942, 85.
9. *Time,* December 7, 1942, 13; January 18, 1943, 45; and March 22, 1943, 23.
10. *Washington Post,* January 14, 1942, 13; *New York Times,* January 21, 1942, 15; and *New York Times Magazine,* November 15, 1942, 14.
11. *Successful Farming,* August 1942, 35; *American Farm Youth,* December 1942, 25; *Winterset Madisonian,* September 2, 1942, 1; and *Winterset Boomerang,* 1943.
12. *Wallaces' Farmer,* July 11, 1942, 3; and *Farm Journal,* October 1942, 40.
13. *Successful Farming,* November 1942, 74; March 1943, 67; February 1944, 88; and March 1944, 99.
14. *Parents,* February 1943, 26; and October 1942, 20.
15. *New York Times,* May 8, 1942, 42.
16. *Los Angeles Times,* March 14, 1943, 5.
17. *New York Times,* December 1, 1942, 27.
18. *Los Angeles Times,* October 10, 1942, 5/part 2; and October 18, 1942, 1/City News.
19. *Saturday Evening Post,* March 13, 1943, 86; June 5, 1943, 97; and July 24, 1943, 76.
20. *New York Times,* February 12, 1942, 13; July 22, 1944, 28; August 16, 1944, 1; and August 18, 1944, 15.
21. *Education for Victory,* September 4, 1944, 5.
22. *Education for Victory,* November 20, 1944, 23; *Life,* June 5, 1944, 67, 68, and 69; and *Newsweek,* April 16, 1945, 52; and July 2, 1945, 91.
23. Tuttle, *"Daddy's Gone to War,"* 123; and Heather Hatch, "Homefront Arizona: A Photo Essay," *Journal of Arizona History* 36, no. 4 (Winter 1995): 394.
24. *New York Times Magazine,* December 6, 1942, 32.
25. *Saturday Evening Post,* February 7, 1942, 48; and April 17, 1943, 30.
26. *Life,* January 18, 1943, 108.
27. *Des Moines Tribune,* June 15, 1942, 1; and July 3, 1942, 1.
28. *Los Angeles Times,* June 19, 1942, 10; *Los Angeles Times,* June 18, 1942, B; *New York Times,* October 2, 1942, 11; *Newsweek,* June 29, 1942, 37; *Life,* July 20, 1942, 77 and 78; and *Los Angeles Times,* July 3, 1942, 1.
29. *Education for Victory,* August 21, 1944, 2; State Historical Society of Iowa, WWII Homefront Activities #11343, folder #1; *Des Moines Register,* January 17, 1945; *Red Oak Sun,* September 28, 1944, 1; *Iowa Farm Bureau Spokesman,* January 13, 1945, 1; and *Kossuth County Advance,* December 14, 1944, 1.
30. Richard Collier, *The Road to Pearl Harbor: 1941,* 2 and 3; Rayness Minns, *Bombers and Mash: The Domestic Front, 1939–1945,* 86; Robert Kee, *1945: The World We Fought For,* 37; and Lewis A. Erenberg and Susan E. Hirsch, *The War in American Consciousness: Society and Consciousness during World War II,* 17.
31. Paul Casdorph, *Let the Good Times Roll: Life at Home in America during World War II,* 81; Mary Martha Thomas, *Riveting and Rationing in Dixie: Alabama Women*

and the Second World War, 96; and Carey L. Draeger, "Use It All; Wear It Out; Make It Do; or Go Without!" *Michigan History Magazine* (September/October 1994): 48 and 49.

32. Ann Starett, "Rationing Is Women's Job," *Independent Woman* (May 1942), 137 and 138; Duis and LaFrance, *We've Got a Job to Do: Chicagoans and World War II,* 5; *Des Moines Register,* May 4, 1943, 7; *Time,* June 21, 1943, 64; Karen Anderson, *Wartime Women: Sex Roles, Family Relations, and the Status of Women during World War II,* 87; and Doris Weatherford, *American Women and World War II,* 216, 206, and 215.

33. *Saturday Evening Post,* September 4, 1943, 40.

34. Draeger, "Use It All," 49.

35. *Los Angeles Times:* February 21, 1943, 6; February 25, 1943, 5; and February 28, 1943, 6.

36. *Time,* May 11, 1942, 22; and *New York Times,* March 30, 1943, 11.

37. *Des Moines Tribune,* April 30, 1942, 28; and May 6, 1942, and Draeger, "Use It All," 41.

38. *Good Housekeeping,* May 1942, 160; and *Saturday Evening Post,* March 6, 1943, 57.

39. *Honolulu Star Tribune,* March 11, 1942, 1; and *Los Angeles Times,* March 7, 1943, 3/part II.

40. *New York Times,* May 11, 1943, 8; and July 14, 1944, 28.

41. Colorado Historical Society, *The Victory Years, The 1940s,* 26, 27, and 28.

42. *Education for Victory,* June 15, 1942, 17.

43. *Education for Victory,* March 3, 1943, 28; and May 3, 1943, 2; Duane K. Hale, "Uncle Sam's Warriors: American Indians in World War II," *Chronicles of Oklahoma* 69, no. 4 (Winter 1993): 409; and *Saturday Evening Post,* April 25, 1942, 100.

44. Charles Osgood, *Defending Baltimore against Enemy Attack: A Boyhood Year during World War II,* 16 and 123.

45. *Education for Victory,* January 20, 1944, 13 and 18.

46. *Education for Victory,* June 4, 1945, 23.

47. *Parents,* March 1945, 30 and 31.

Chapter 4: Junior Commandos

1. *Des Moines Register,* December 14, 1941, 1; and *Los Angeles Times,* December 8, 1941, 1/City News.

2. *Honolulu Star-Bulletin,* December 13, 1941, 6.

3. *Atlanta Constitution,* December 15, 1941, 2; and *Time,* May 11, 1942, 34.

4. Franklin D. Roosevelt Presidential Library, President's Personal File, PPF 200B, Public Reaction, file December 8, 1941 (John Barry School); and *Successful Farming,* September 1944, 8.

5. Pamela Riney-Kehrberg, *Childhood on the Farm: Work, Play, and Coming of Age in the Midwest,* 26 and 27.

6. Osgood, *Defending Baltimore against Enemy Attack,* 49 and 50.

7. *New York Times,* December 12, 1943, 16; *Parents,* December 1942, 64; *Popular*

Mechanics, August 1944, 92 and 93; and *Parents*, November 1943, 68.

8. *Newsweek*, May 15, 1944, 8.

9. *Parents*, July 1942, 26 and 27.

10. *Washington Post*, January 15, 1942, 13.

11. *Washington Post*, January 19, 1942, 9; and *Saturday Evening Post*, April 4, 1942, 64.

12. *Good Housekeeping*, February 1944.

13. Diane E. Levin and Nancy Carlsson-Paige, *The War Play Dilemma: What Every Parent and Teacher Needs to Know*, 54 and 55.

14. *New York Times*, March 3, 1943, 14; *Education for Victory*, September 1, 1943, 1; *Life*, May 17, 1943, 45; *Education for Victory*, February 3, 1944, 1; and December 15, 1943, 13; and *Saturday Evening Post*, May 30, 1942, 98; and July 11, 1942, 82.

15. State Historical Society of Iowa Archives, World War II Photographs, folder #3; and *New Yorker*, September 5, 1942, 10.

16. *Good Housekeeping*, December 1942, 106, 107, and 108; and *New York Times*, November 28, 1943, 3.

17. *New York Times*, November 8, 1941, 18.

18. *Parents*, December 1941, 78.

19. Juliet Gardiner in association with the Imperial War Museum, *The Children's War: The Second World War through the Eyes of the Children of Britain*, 100; and Sally Alderson, *War All Over the World: Childhood Memories of World War II from Twenty-three Countries*, 200.

20. *Good Housekeeping*, December 1942, 107.

21. *Popular Mechanics*, January 1945, 76 and 77; and *Education for Victory*, July 1, 1942, 8.

22. Franklin D. Roosevelt Presidential Library, President's Personal File, 200B, container 116, file: October 12, 1942/pro A-F/letters from a teacher named William Brody of class 5B, P.S. 75, Brooklyn, New York.

23. *Los Angeles Times*, January 30, 1942, B; and David M. Oshinsky, *Polio: An American Story*, 68 and 69.

24. *House and Garden*, November 1944, 56.

25. *Los Angeles Times*, January 30, 1942, B; *House and Garden*, December 1943, 53; and *Life*, October 4, 1943, 43.

26. *Newsweek*, November 22, 1943, 62; Wilma Davis Gundy, "Snapshots from Old Soddy: A Farm Girl's Life on the Eastern Colorado Plains in the 1930s and '40s," *Colorado Heritage* (Autumn 2004): 9; and *Los Angeles Times*, December 5, 1942, 11.

27. Daryl Webb, "Scooters, Skates, and Dolls: Toys against Delinquency in Milwaukee," *Wisconsin Magazine of History* (Summer 2004): 12; and State Historical Society of Iowa Archives, World War II Photographs, folder #3 (dated Des Moines, Iowa; March 1945).

28. *Popular Mechanics*, October 1944, 105; *New York Times*, November 12, 1943, 26; *Popular Mechanics*, April 1943, 89; and *Los Angeles Times*, December 6, 1942, 10.

29. *House and Garden*, November 1942; and *Popular Mechanics*, January 1944, 113; October 1944, 97; and June 1944.

30. *Life,* December 27, 1943, 87; and December 13, 1943, 105.

31. *New York Times,* November 7, 1941, 22; West and Petrik, *Small Worlds,* 159; *New York Times Magazine,* July 11, 1943, 23; and Kirk, *Earning Their Stripes,* 36.

32. *Parents,* April 1941, 17; May 1941, 7; July 1942, 40; and August 1945, 17; and West and Petrik, 159.

33. *Parents,* December 1942, 102; and *Des Moines Tribune,* March 11, 1942, 20.

34. *New York Times,* November 21, 1943, 14.

35. *Life,* January 11, 1943, 94 and 95.

36. *New York Times,* December 1, 1943, 23.

37. *Washington Post,* July 23, 1942, 16.

38. *Parents,* December 1942, 28 and 29; and *Successful Farming,* December 1943, 53.

39. American Heritage Center, University of Wyoming Archives, Heart Mountain Relocation Center Records, accession number 9804, box 2, folder 1: *Heart Mountain Sentinel,* December 5, 1942, 6.

40. American Heritage Center, University of Wyoming Archives, Estelle Ishigo, Photographs and Drawings 1928–1972, accession number 10368; and Emmy E. Werner, *Through the Eyes of Innocents: Children Witness World War II,* 89.

41. American Heritage Center, University of Wyoming Archives, clippings file: W893WII-rc-hm. World War II—Relocation Camp—Heart Mountain, letter dated July 6, 1993, photos from class of '47.

42. *Good Housekeeping,* September 1942, 17.

43. *Saturday Evening Post,* July 18, 1942, 49.

44. Werner, *Through the Eyes of Innocents,* 77 and 78.

Chapter 5: Soldier Citizens

1. *Los Angeles Times,* December 27, 1941, 1; and February 7, 1942, 16/part 1.

2. Davis, *FDR: The War President,* 713; and *Education for Victory,* September 1, 1942.

3. *Parents,* January 1942, 26; and June 1942, 34.

4. *Time,* June 15, 1942, 15; *New York Times,* March 3, 1943, 14; and March 4, 1943, 13; *Saturday Evening Post*, March 11, 1944, 112; *Time,* September 11, 1944, 72; and *Life,* May 17, 1943, 45.

5. Shelton Stromquist, *Solidarity and Survival: An Oral History of Iowa Labor in the Twentieth Century,* 125; William L. O'Neill, *A Democracy at War: America's Fight at Home and Abroad in World War II,* 214; David Hinshaw, *The Home Front,* 185 and 186; and Nelson Lichtenstein, *Labor's War at Home: The CIO in World War II,* 5 and 6.

6. O'Neill, *A Democracy at War,* 75; *Iowa Business,* October 1946, 22; *Des Moines Tribune,* January 8, 1944, 1; and Joel Seidman, *American Labor from Defense to Reconversion,* 153; Richard Macias, "'We All Had a Cause': Kansas City's Bomber Plant, 1941–1945," *Kansas History: A Journal of the Central Plains* 28, no. 4 (Winter 2005–2006): 253.

7. *Iowa Bystander,* July 17, 1941, 1; and August 7, 1941, 1.

8. *Iowa Bystander,* April 9, 1942, 1. U.S. Rubber Company managed Des Moines

Ordnance Plant—an example of a GOCO defense plant—government owned, company operated.

9. *Iowa Bystander,* February 15, 1945, 3.

10. Stromquist, *Solidarity and Survival,* 246, 248, and 249.

11. Seidman, *American Labor,* 165; Karen Tucker Anderson, "Last Hired, First Fired: Black Women Workers during World War II," *Journal of American History* 69 (June 1982): 82–85; *Des Moines Tribune,* August 19, 1943; *Des Moines Register,* June 1, 1944; and November 25, 1944, 1.

12. O'Neill, *A Democracy at War,* 249.

13. Margaret Chase Smith Library, "Washington and You": Statements, Speeches to 77th Congress, 1941–1942, vol. 1 (28 August 1941); and Pat Koehler, "Reminiscence: The Women Ship Builders of World War II," *Oregon Historical Quarterly* 91, no. 3 (Fall 1990): 285.

14. *Time,* June 15, 1942, 15.

15. Natusuki Aruga, "'An' Finish School': Child Labor during World War II," *Labor History* 29 (Fall 1988): 498 and 517; *Burlington Hawk-Eye Gazette,* November 17, 1942, 2; and Polenberg, *War and Society,* 79.

16. Wolf, *Our Children Face War,* 70 and 83; Gerhard Rempel, *Hitler's Children: The Hitler Youth and the SS,* 137; and *Collier's,* April 24, 1943, 18, 19, and 56.

17. *Iowa Farm Bureau Spokesman,* August 26, 1944, 4.

18. *New York Times,* April 12, 1942, 18; *Life,* September 27, 1943, 109; *Los Angeles Times,* November 22, 1942, 1/Women's Section; *Washington Post,* March 15, 1942, 2; *New York Times Magazine,* March 7, 1943, 19; *New York Times,* April 3, 1943, 12; *Washington Post,* April 24, 1942, 12; and *Life,* June 15, 1942, 73.

19. *Los Angeles Times,* November 22, 1942, 9; *Life,* September 14, 1942, 93; November 16, 1942, 69; and January 3, 1944, 33.

20. *New York Times Magazine,* September 20, 1942, 24; and *Education for Victory,* September 1, 1943, 1.

21. *New York Times,* January 14, 1945, 34; and *Iowa Agriculturalist,* February 1943.

22. *Successful Farmer,* March 1943, 74.

23. *Wallaces' Farmer,* July 11, 1942, cover.

24. *Wallaces' Farmer,* September 18, 1943, 26.

25. New York State Archives, Laurence I. Hewes Jr. collection, box 1, correspondence 1942–1971.

26. *Successful Farming,* January 1943, 4.

27. *Wallaces' Farmer,* June 3, 1944, 17.

28. War-Peace Pamphlets, no. 3. "Food as an Implement of War: The Responsibilities of Farmers" by Joseph S. Davis, Food Research Institute, Stanford University (November 1943); and *Successful Farming,* November 1942.

29. *Successful Farming,* August 1943, 70.

30. Viviana A. Zelizer, *Pricing the Priceless Child: The Changing Social Value of Children,* 77; David I. Macleod, *The Age of the Child: Children in America, 1890–1920,* 7 and 8; Pamela Riney-Kehrberg, "Helping Ma and Helping Pa: Iowa's Turn-of-

the-Century Farm Children," *Annals of Iowa* 59 (Spring 2000), 126; and *Iowa Farm Bureau Spokesman,* June 12, 1943, 5.

31. *Successful Farming,* November 1942, 74; *Education for Victory,* no. 4, April 15, 1942, 2; and O'Brien, "Kansas at War," 18.

32. *Wallaces' Farmer,* June 19, 1943, 1.

33. *New York Times,* July 10, 1943, 16L.

34. New York State Archives, Farm Labor Correspondence, box A4355–78, folder Tivoli Camp ("Farmerette Fanfare" vol. 1, no. 5), 4.

35. New York State Archives, Farm Labor Correspondence, box A4355–78, folder Tivoli Camp ("Farmerette Fanfare" vol. 1, no. 5), 4; and New York State Archives, Farm Labor Correspondence, box A4348–78, folder Wa-Waq.

36. New York State Archives, Farm Labor Correspondence, box A4348–78, folder Mo-Moq.

37. New York State Archives, Farm Labor Correspondence, box A4348–78, folder Radio Programs.

38. New York State Archives, Farm Labor Correspondence, box A4348–78, folder Cb-Chaz.

39. New York State Archives, Farm Labor Correspondence, box A4348–78, folder Ge-Gn.

40. New York State Archives, Farm Labor Correspondence, box A4348–78, folder Wa-Waq.

41. New York State Archives, Farm Labor Correspondence, box A4355–78, folder F.C.V.C. Administrative.

42. New York State Archives, State Education Department (1942–1945), 15080–78, folder 41 Farm Cadet Victory Corp.

43. New York State Archives, Farm Labor Correspondence, letter dated January 30, 1945.

44. *Education for Victory,* February 3, 1944, 1.

45. *Education for Victory,* June 1, 1942, 15; and March 1, 1943, 3.

46. *Education for Victory,* July 1, 1943, 1.

47. *Successful Farming,* December 1942, 23; and *Iowa Parent-Teacher Association,* June-July 1943, 39.

48. *Wallaces' Farmer,* April 18, 1942, 7; and August 8, 1942, 8; and *Iowa Bureau Farmer,* June 1942, 7 and 14.

49. New York State Archives, Farm Labor Correspondence, box A4355–78, folder Tivoli Camp (Farmerette Fanfare/Girls! Girls! Girls! August 6, 1944, vol. 1, no. 5).

50. New York State Archives, Farm Labor Correspondence, box A4355–78, folder Supervisors—1944.

51. *American Farm Youth,* September 1945, 22.

52. *American Farm Youth,* March 1945, 25; and *Successful Farming,* September 1945, 92.

53. *Iowa Farm Bureau Spokesman,* July 29, 1944, 11.

54. *Wallaces' Farmer,* August 4, 1945, 4; June 2, 1945, 4; and December 2, 1944, 6.

Chapter 6: War Waifs

1. Werner, *Through the Eyes of Innocents,* 94.

2. New York State Archives, President's Committee for Congested Production Areas, pamphlet, "President's Committee for Congested Production Areas," December 1944; Kennedy, 747 and 748; and Riney-Kehrberg, *Childhood on the Farm,* 209.

3. Samuel Grafton, *An American Diary,* entry dated June 28, 1941.

4. *Los Angeles Times,* February 8, 1943, 4/part 2.

5. *New York Times,* April 6, 1943, 23.

6. *New York Times,* September 12, 1943, 1/Real Estate.

7. Lionel Kimble Jr., "I Too Serve America: African-American Women War Workers in Chicago, 1940–1945," *Journal of the Illinois State Historical Society* 93, no. 4 (Winter 2000–2001): 426 and 427.

8. "Michigan Goes to War," *Michigan History Magazine* (March/April 1993): 34, 35, 36, 37, and 38.

9. Richard Overy, "The Successes of American Mobilization," in Mark A. Stoler and Melanie S. Gustafson, eds., *Major Problems in the History of World War II,* 63 and 71; and Larry Lankton, "Autos to Armaments: Detroit Becomes the Arsenal of Democracy," *Michigan History Magazine* (November/December 1991): 48.

10. Tuttle, *"Daddy's Gone to War,"* 64 and 65.

11. Beverly Russell, "World War II Boomtown: Hastings and the Naval Ammunition Depot," *Nebraska History* 76, no. 2–3 (Summer–Fall 1995): 78, 80, and 82.

12. Rudy Pearson, "'A Menace to the Neighborhood': Housing and African Americans in Portland, 1941–1945," *Oregon Historical Quarterly* 102, no. 2 (Summer 2001): 159, 160, 171, 176.

13. John Gurda, "Profits and Patriotism: Milwaukee Industry in World War II," *Wisconsin Magazine of History* 78, no. 1 (Autumn 1994): 24.

14. Tuttle, *"Daddy's Gone to War,"* 168 and 171.

15. Karen L. Riley, *Schools behind Barbed Wire: The Untold Story of Wartime Internment and the Children of Arrested Enemy Aliens,* 6.

16. Stoler and Gustafson, eds., "Major Problems in the History of World War II" ["Wartime Internment"], *Journal of American History* 77, no. 2 (September 1990): 569 and 575.

17. Judy Kutulas, *The American Civil Liberties Union and the Making of Modern Liberalism, 1930–1960,* 116 and 117; and *Los Angeles Times,* February 9, 1942, 3; March 4, 1942, B; April 15, 1942, 10; and April 16, 1942, 1.

18. Richardson, *Reflections of Pearl Harbor,* 166.

19. Robert Asahina, *Just Americans: How Japanese Americans Won a War at Home and Abroad. The Story of the 100th Battalion/442d Regimental Combat Team in World War II,* 26; and *Los Angeles Times,* September 26, 1942, 1.

20. American Heritage Archives, box 2, *Heart Mountain Sentinel,* November 14, 1942, 3; November 28, 1942, 2; 5 December 1942, 6; and January 1, 1943, 1.

21. *Heart Mountain Sentinel,* April 24, 1943; and May 1, 1943, 8.

22. *Heart Mountain Sentinel,* May 29, 1943, 8; July 24, 1943, 3; March 18, 1944, 3;

August 21, 1943, 3; and September 2, 1944, 3; and Asahina, *Just Americans*, 112.

23. Riley, *Schools behind Barbed Wire*, 1; *Heart Mountain Sentinel*, September 11, 1943, 6; and August 26, 1944, 8; Werner, *Through the Eyes of Innocents*, 221; and *Education for Victory*, November 16, 1942, 7 and 8.

24. *Heart Mountain Sentinel*, May 1, 1943, 8; and April 1, 1944, 8; and Taylor Branch, *At Canaan's Edge: America in the King Years, 1965–1968*, 138.

25. Kutulas, *The American Civil Liberties*, 116 and 117; and Werner, *Through the Eyes of Innocents*, 99.

26. *Heart Mountain Sentinel*, June 26, 1943, 5.

27. Lauren Kessler, *Stubborn Twig: Three Generations in the Life of a Japanese American Family*, 232 and 233.

28. *Phylon: The Atlanta University Review of Race and Culture* 4, no. 2 (1943), 130.

Chapter 7: Zoot Suits and Victory Girls

1. American Heritage Center, University of Wyoming Archives, Heart Mountain Relocation Center Records 1943–1945, accession number 9804, box 1, folder 8.

2. *Saturday Evening Post*, April 29, 1944, 28, 29, 96, and 98.

3. *Life*, December 20, 1943, 96 and 97.

4. *New York Times*, November 8, 1942, 10; and *New York Times Magazine*, March 19, 1944, 23.

5. *New York Times Magazine*, November 8, 1942, 10; September 20, 1942, 24; and July 12, 1942, 22; *Newsweek*, November 9, 1942, 27; and *Time*, April 12, 1943, 25.

6. *Life*, December 20, 1943, 96 and 97; and June 12, 1944, 68 and 69.

7. Kenneth Paul O'Brien and Lynn Hudson Parsons, *The Home-Front War: World War II and American Society*, 119 and 120.

8. Miriam Frank, Marilyn Ziebarth, and Connie Field, *The Life and Times of Rosie the Riveter.*

9. Mauricio Mazon, *The Zoot-Suit Riots: The Psychology of Symbolic Annihilation*, 9.

10. *Newsweek*, August 24, 1942, 34 and 35; and *Los Angeles Times*, October 15, 1942, 1/City News.

11. *Los Angeles Times*, November 24, 1942, 1.

12. Tom Sitton, *Los Angeles Transformed: Fletcher Bowron's Urban Reform Revival, 1938–1953*, 52; Eduardo Obregon Pagan, *Murder at the Sleepy Lagoon: Zoot Suits, Race, and Riot in Wartime L.A.*, 44; and Jon Savage, *Teenage: The Creation of Youth Culture*, 396.

13. *New York Times*, June 11, 1943, 21.

14. Pagan, *Murder at the Sleepy Lagoon*, 117; and Savage, *Teenage*, 396.

15. *Life*, September 21, 1942, 44 and 45.

16. Patty Loew, "The Back of the Homefront: Black and American Indian Women in Wisconsin during World War II," *Wisconsin Magazine of History* 82, no. 2 (Winter 1998–1999): 94 and 95.

17. John Hersey, editor, *Ralph Ellison: A Collection of Critical Essays,* 68; and *Newsweek,* June 21, 1943, 40.
18. *Newsweek,* June 21, 1943, 25.
19. Pagan, *Murder at the Sleepy Lagoon,* 36.
20. *Newsweek,* August 24, 1942, 34 and 35; and *Los Angeles Times,* August 3, 1942, 1.
21. *Los Angeles Times,* August 10, 1942, 1.
22. *Los Angeles Times,* October 10, 1942, 1.
23. *Newsweek,* June 21, 1943, 35 and 38; and Pagan, *Murder at the Sleepy Lagoon,* 180.
24. *New York Times,* November 20, 1942; and March 14, 1943, 1/section 2; and Pearson, "A Menace to the Neighborhood," 62.
25. *Life,* January 1, 1945, 2; and June 11, 1945, 91 and 92; and *Successful Farming,* January 1946.
26. *Saturday Evening Post,* April 24, 1943, 90.
27. *New York Times Magazine,* August 5, 1944, 16 and 32.
28. *Life,* January 10, 1944, back cover.
29. *Time,* October 30, 1941, 38.
30. Greene, *Once Upon a Town: The Miracle of the North Platte Canteen,* 94 and 95.
31. O'Brien and Parsons, *The Home-Front War,* 122; *Life,* December 20, 1943, 102; and O'Neill, *A Democracy at War,* 264 and 265.
32. *Life,* December 20, 1943, 96, 97, and 102; and *Time,* March 29, 1943, 46.
33. *Life,* August 31, 1942, 41; and *Time,* December 8, 1941, 36.
34. *Newsweek,* January 22, 1944, 38.
35. *Life,* December 11, 1944, 91, 92, 95, 96, and 98.
36. *Parents,* August 1944, 31; New York State Archives, New York State War Council, advisory correspondence, roll number 7, letter dated March 27, 1945; Franklin D. Roosevelt Library, OF 4675, World War II, Miscellaneous 1944, letter dated September 15, 1944.
37. *New York Times,* January 7, 1945, 16 and 17.
38. *New York Times,* March 18, 1944, 15.

Chapter 8: Gold Stars

1. *New York Times,* December 3, 1944, 30.
2. *New York Times,* December 23, 1944, 4.
3. Franklin D. Roosevelt Presidential Library, Correspondence, container 120, file December 24, 1943.
4. Franklin D. Roosevelt Presidential Library, President Roosevelt's Personal File, PPF 200B, Public Reaction, file December 8, 1941.
5. *New York Times,* August 17, 1944, 7.
6. Sharon E. McHaney, "Michigan Remembers 'The Longest Day,'" *Michigan History Magazine* (May/June 1994): 40.
7. *Life,* January 5, 1942, 69; and April 20, 1942, 5; and *Saturday Evening Post,* May 22, 1943, 69.

8. O'Neill, *A Democracy at War,* 87; and American Jewish Archives, manuscript no. 202, JCRC, box 2.

9. *Los Angeles Times,* September 16, 1942, 1; *New York Times,* December 9, 1943, 1; and September 19, 1943, 10B; Richard Carlton Haney, "'When Is Daddy Coming Home?': An American Family during World War II," *Wisconsin Magazine of History* (Winter 2004–2005): 38 and 39; *New York Times,* October 7, 1943, 1; and Kennedy, 635.

10. Margaret Chase Smith Library, "Washington and You," vol. 1, speech, June 26, 1941; *Time,* September 7, 1942, 26; and January 25, 1943, 57.

11. Margaret Chase Smith Library, "Washington and You," vol. 3, May 3, 1945.

12. *Atlanta Constitution,* January 1, 1942, 15; *Life,* October 5, 1942, 53; and October 4, 1943, 81; and *Time,* September 6, 1943, 24.

13. *Newsweek,* May 15, 1944, 3; *Life,* February 21, 1944, 109; and *Los Angeles Times,* May 28, 1942, 1.

14. *Life,* August 16, 1943, 67; *Des Moines Tribune,* June 16, 1942, 3; and *Saturday Evening Post,* February 5, 1944, 47.

15. *New York Times,* December 27, 1941, 10.

16. *Parents,* March 1942, 36; *Washington Post,* January 9, 1942, 17; January 10, 1942, 11; and March 25, 1942, 13.

17. *Better Homes and Gardens,* April 1942, 64 and 65.

18. *New York Times,* April 19, 1944, 25; and April 25, 1944, 6; *Saturday Evening Post,* March 28, 1942, 9; and *Education for Victory,* August 3, 1944, 3.

19. American Jewish Archives, Samuel S. Aronson, manuscript no. 625, box 1 of 3, series A, Correspondence, 1941–1948, folder 3.

20. Franklin D. Roosevelt Presidential Library, personal, file S. For the "Teen Age Draft Bill," see Paul A. Frisch, "Conscription (U.S.)" in James Ciment, ed., *The Home Front Encyclopedia: United States, Britain, and Canada in World Wars I and II,* vol. 2: *World War II.*

21. Greene, *Once Upon a Town,* 61, 141, 175, 176, and 180.

22. O'Brien, "Kansas at War," 14.

23. *New York Times,* December 13, 1942, 25; and December 20, 1942, 12.

24. *New York Times,* July 16, 1943, 19; *Life,* July 26, 1943, 35; and *New York Times,* January 20, 1944, 6.

25. *Time,* October 2, 1944, 25.

26. *Newsweek,* August 13, 1945, 24 and 25; and *Time,* August 13, 1945, 18.

27. Suzanne Mettler, *Soldiers to Citizens: The G.I. Bill and the Making of the Greatest Generation,* 15 and 16; *Life,* November 13, 1944, 103; and *Time,* June 11, 1945, 60.

28. Calvin L. Christman, ed. (collected by Susan Johnson Hadler and Ann Bennett Mix), *Lost in the Victory: Reflections of American War Orphans of World War II,* xi. As Jeff Ward comments (in the text), "war orphan" is an interesting term and "really not fair to the woman, because it's as if both parents were killed in the war."

29. *Parents,* October 1945, 28.

30. *New York Times Magazine,* May 7, 1944, 16; and April 9, 1944, 29; *Newsweek,* July 2, 1945, 26; and *Life,* December 11, 1944, 4.

31. *Life,* August 13, 1945, 13.

32. Asahina, *Just Americans,* 231.

33. Tuttle, *"Daddy's Gone to War,"* 44 and 48; and Gilbert, *The Day the War Ended.*

34. Haney, "'When Is Daddy Coming Home?'" 38.

35. Christman, *Lost in the Victory,* table of contents.

36. Franklin D. Roosevelt Presidential Library, Eleanor Roosevelt Papers, Condolence Correspondence.

Conclusion: The Forgotten Generation

1. *New York Times,* August 15, 1945, 5.

2. *New York Times,* August 15, 1945, 1, 3, and 5; *Atlanta Constitution,* August 15, 1945, 1; and *Life,* August 27, 1945, 21, 24, and 26.

3. *Atlanta Constitution,* August 15, 1945, 7.

4. Mullener, *War Stories,* 29.

Bibliography

Children are pivotal to how a culture defines itself and its future.

—Paula Fass, *Children of a New World* (2007)

Archival Sources

American Heritage Center, University of Wyoming, Laramie
American Jewish Archives, Cincinnati
Des Moines Public Library, Des Moines, Iowa
Iowa State University Archive, Ames, Iowa
National Archives, Washington, D.C.
New York State Archives, Albany, New York
Franklin D. Roosevelt Presidential Library, Hyde Park, New York
Margaret Chase Smith Library, Skowhegan, Maine
State Historical Society of Iowa, Des Moines

Articles and Books

Aapola, Sinikka; Marnina Gonick and Anita Harris, eds. (with Jo Campling as consultant editor). *Young Femininity: Girlhood, Power, and Social Change.* New York: Palgrave Macmillan, 2005.

Abrahamson, James. *The American Home Front: Revolutionary War, Civil War, World War I, World War II.* Washington, D.C.: National Defense University Press, 1983.

Albrecht, Donald, ed. *World War II and the American Dream: How Wartime Building Changed a Nation.* Cambridge, Mass.: MIT Press, 1995.

Alderson, Sally (compiler). *War All Over the World: Childhood Memories of World War II from Twenty-three Countries.* Switzerland: Salenca Press, 2003.

Allen, Thomas B. *Pearl Harbor: American and Japanese Survivors Tell Their Stories.* Washington, D.C.: National Geographic Society, 2001.

Aly, Gotz. *Hitler's Beneficiaries: Plunder, Racial War, and the Nazi Welfare State.* Translated by Jefferson Chase. New York: Metropolitan Books/Henry Holt, 2005.

Ambrose, Stephen A. *Americans at War.* Jackson: University Press of Mississippi, 1997.

———. *Citizen Soldiers: The U.S. Army from the Normandy Beaches to the Bulge to the Surrender of Germany, June 7, 1944–May 7, 1945.* New York: Simon and Schuster, 1997.

Anderson, Karen. *Wartime Women: Sex Roles, Family Relations, and the Status of Women during World War II.* Westport, Conn.: Greenwood Press, 1981.

Anderson, Karen Tucker. "Last Hired, First Fired: Black Women Workers during World War II." *Journal of American History* 69 (June 1982).

Aruga, Natusuki. "'An' Finish School': Child Labor during World War II." *Labor History* 29 (Fall 1988).

Asahina, Robert. *Just Americans: How Japanese Americans Won a War at Home and Abroad. The Story of the 100th Battalion/442d Regimental Combat Team in World War II.* New York: Gotham Books, 2006.

Baruch, Dorothy. *You, Your Children, and War.* New York: D. Appleton-Century, 1943.

Bettis, Pamela J., and Natalie G. Adams, eds. *Geographies of Girlhood: Identities In-Between.* Mahwah, N.J.: Lawrence Erlbaum Associates, 2005.

Black, Wallace B., and Jean F. Blashfield. *Pearl Harbor!* New York: Crestwood House, 1991.

Blum, John M. *V Was for Victory: Politics and American Culture during World War II.* New York: Harcourt Brace Jovanovich, 1976.

Boot, Max. *War Made New: Technology, Warfare, and the Course of History, 1500 to Today.* New York: Gotham Books, 2006.

Borgwardt, Elizabath. *A New Deal for the World: America's Vision for Human Rights.* Cambridge, Mass.: Belknap Press of Harvard University Press, 2005.

Branch, Taylor. *At Canaan's Edge: America in the King Years, 1965–1968.* New York: Simon and Schuster, 2006.

Braverman, Jordan. *To Hasten the Homecoming: How Americans Fought World War II through the Media.* New York: Madison Books, 1996.

Brinkley, Douglas, ed. *World War II: The Axis Assault, 1939–1942.* New York: Henry Holt, 2003.

———. *The World War II Memorial: A Grateful Nation Remembers.* Washington, D.C.: Smithsonian Books, 2007.

Brittin, Burdick H. "We Four Ensigns (Being an account by one of them of the Pearl Harbor attack)." *Proceedings of the United States Naval Institute* (December 1966).

Brokaw, Tom. *The Greatest Generation.* New York: Random House, 1998.

Campbell, D'Ann. *Women at War with America: Private Lives in a Patriotic Era.* Cambridge, Mass.: Harvard University Press, 1984.

Cardozier, V. R. *The Mobilization of the United States in World War II: How the Government, Military, and Industry Prepared for War.* Jefferson, N.C.: McFarland, 1995.

Carr, Lowell Juilliard, and James Edson Stermer. *Willow Run: A Study of Industrialization and Cultural Inadequacy.* New York: Harper and Brothers, 1952.

Casdorph, Paul. *Let the Good Times Roll: Life at Home in America during World War II.* New York: Paragon House, 1989.

Cavnes, Max Parvin. *The Hoosier Community at War.* Bloomington: Indiana University Press, 1961.

Chirhart, Ann Short. *Torches of Light: Georgia Teachers and the Coming of the Modern South.* Athens: University of Georgia Press, 2005.

Christman, Calvin L., ed. Collected by Susan Johnson Hadler and Ann Bennett Mix. *Lost in the Victory: Reflections of American War Orphans of World War II.* Denton: University of North Texas Press, 1998.

Ciment, James, ed. *The Home Front Encyclopedia: United States, Britain, and Canada in World Wars I and II.* Volume 2: *World War II.* Santa Barbara, Calif.: ABC/Clio, 2007.

Clark, Blake. *Remember Pearl Harbor!* New York: Modern Age Books, 1942.

Cohen, Stan. *V for Victory: America's Home Front during World War II.* Missoula, Mont.: Pictorial Histories, 1991.

Collier, Richard. *1940: The World in Flames.* London: Hamish Hamilton, 1979.

———. *The Road to Pearl Harbor: 1941.* New York: Bonanza Books, 1984.

Colorado Historical Society. *The Victory Years, the 1940s.* Denver: Public Service Company of Colorado, 1995.

Cowan, Lore. *Children of the Resistance.* New York: Meredith, 1969.

Davis, Kenneth S. *FDR: The War President, 1940–1943.* New York: Random House, 2000.

De Ras, Marion, and Mieke Lunenberg, eds. *Girls, Girlhood, and Girls' Studies in Transition.* Amsterdam: Het Spinhuis, 1993.

Dooley, Patricia. "Gopher Ordnance Works: Condemnation, Construction, and Community Response." *Minnesota History* 49 (Summer 1985).

Draeger, Carey L. "Use It All; Wear It Out; Make It Do; or Go Without!" *Michigan History Magazine* (September/October 1994).

Duis, Perry R., and Scott LaFrance. *We've Got a Job to Do: Chicagoans and World War II.* Chicago: Chicago Historical Society, 1992.

Dunnahoo, Terry. *Pearl Harbor: America Enters the War.* New York: Franklin Watts, 1991.

"Editorial: The War and After." *Understanding the Child* 12, no. 2 (June 1943).

Erenberg, Lewis A., and Susan E. Hirsch. *The War in American Consciousness: Society and Consciousness during World War II.* Chicago: University of Chicago Press, 1996.

Evans, Richard J. *The Third Reich in Power, 1933–1939.* New York: Penguin, 2005.

Ferguson, Niall. *The War of the World: Twentieth-Century Conflict and the Descent of the West.* New York: Penguin, 2006.

Figes, Eva. *Little Eden: A Child at War.* New York: Persea Books, 1978.

Fleming, Thomas. *The New Dealers' War: F.D.R. and the War within World War II.* New York: Basic Books, 2001.

Frank, Miriam, Marilyn Ziebarth, and Connie Field. *The Life and Times of Rosie the Riveter.* Emeryville, Calif.: Clarity Educational Productions, 1982.

Fromkin, David. *In the Time of the Americans: FDR, Truman, Eisenhower, Marshall, MacArthur—The Generation that Changed America's Role in the World.* New York: Alfred A. Knopf, 1995.

Fuchida, Mitsuo. *From Pearl Harbor to Golgotha.* San Jose, Calif.: Sky Pilots Press, 1957.

Fuchida, Mitsuo (Captain). "I Led the Air Attack on Pearl Harbor." *United States Naval Proceedings* (September 1952).

Fyson, Nance Lui. *Growing Up in the Second World War.* London: Batsford Academic and Educational, 1981.

Gardiner, Juliet. *The Children's War: The Second World War through the Eyes of the Children of Britain.* In association with the Imperial War Museum. London: Portrait, 2005.

Garrigue, Sheila. *All the Children Were Sent Away.* Scarsdale, New York: Bradbury, 1976.

Gilbert, Martin. *The Day the War Ended: May 8, 1945—Victory in Europe.* New York: Henry Holt, 2004.

Goldstein, Donald M., and Katherine V. Dillon, eds. *The Pearl Harbor Papers: Inside the Japanese Plans.* Dulles, Va.: Brassey's, 2000.

Good, Michael. *The Search for Major Plagge: The Nazi Who Saved Jews.* New York: Fordham University Press, 2005.

Graff, Harvey J., ed. *Growing Up in America: Historical Experiences.* Detroit: Wayne State University Press, 1987.

Grafton, Samuel. *An American Diary.* Garden City, N.Y.: Doubleday, Doran, 1943.

Graham, Patricia Albjerg. *Schooling America: How the Public Schools Meet the Nation's Changing Needs.* New York: Oxford University Press, 2005.

Gray, Denver D. "I Remember Pearl Harbor: A Nebraska Army Air Force Officer in the Pacific Theater during World War II." *Nebraska History* 62 (Winter 1981).

Greene, Bob. *Once Upon a Town: The Miracle of the North Platte Canteen.* New York: Perennial, 2003.

Gregory, Chester W. *Women in Defense Work during World War II: An Analysis of the Labor Problem and Women's Rights.* New York: Exposition Press, 1974.

Gruhzit-Hoyt, Olga. *They Also Served: American Women in World War II.* New York: Birch Lane Press, 1995.

Gundy, Wilma Davis. "Snapshots from Old Soddy: A Farm Girl's Life on the Eastern Colorado Plains in the 1930s and '40s." *Colorado Heritage* (Autumn 2004).

Gurda, John. "Profits and Patriotism: Milwaukee Industry in World War II." *Wisconsin Magazine of History* 78, no. 1 (Autumn 1994).

Hale, Duane K. "Uncle Sam's Warriors: American Indians in World War II." *Chronicles of Oklahoma* 69, no. 4 (Winter 1993).

Hall, Donald. *The Farm Summer 1942.* New York: Dial Books, 1994.

Hamby, Alonzo L. *Man of the People: A Life of Harry S Truman.* New York: Oxford University Press, 1995.

Haney, Richard Carlton. "'When Is Daddy Coming Home?': An American Family during World War II." *Wisconsin Magazine of History* (Winter 2004–2005).

Hanson, David. E. "Home-Front Casualties of War Mobilization: Portland Public Schools, 1941–1945," *Oregon Historical Quarterly* 96, nos. 2/3 (Summer-Fall 1995).

Harris, Mark Jonathan, Franklin D. Mitchell, and Steven J. Schechter. *The Home Front: America during World War II.* New York: G. P. Putnam's Sons, 1984.

Hartman, Susan. "Prescriptions for Penelope: Literature on Women's Obligations to Returning World War II Veterans." *Women's Studies* 5 (1978).

Hastings, Max. *Victory in Europe: D-Day to V-E Day.* Boston: Little, Brown, 1985.
Hatch, Heather. "Homefront Arizona: A Photo Essay." *Journal of Arizona History* 36, no. 4 (Winter 1995).
Hawes, Joseph M. *Children between the Wars: American Childhood, 1920–1940.* New York: Twayne, 1997.
Hermand, Jost. *A Hitler Youth in Poland: The Nazis' Program for Evacuating Children during World War II.* Translated by Margot Bettauer Dembo. Evanston, Ill.: Northwestern University Press, 1993.
Hersey, John, ed. *Ralph Ellison: A Collection of Critical Essays.* Englewood Cliffs, N.J.: Prentice Hall, 1974.
Hinshaw, David. *The Home Front.* New York: G. P. Putnam's Sons, 1943.
Honey, Maureen. *Creating Rosie the Riveter: Class, Gender, and Propaganda during World War II.* Amherst: University of Massachusetts Press, 1984.
Horne, Alistair. *A Bundle from Britain.* New York: St. Martin's, 1993.
Horseman, Grace, ed. *Growing Up in the Forties.* London: Constable, 1997.
Hurt, R. Douglas. *The Great Plains during World War II.* Lincoln: University of Nebraska Press, 2008.
Inglis, Ruth. *The Children's War: Evacuation, 1939–1945.* London: Collins, 1989.
Jackson, Carlton. *Who Will Take Our Children? The Story of the Evacuation in Britain, 1939–1945.* London: Methuen, 1985.
Jeffries, John W. *Wartime America: The World War II Home Front.* Chicago: Ivan R. Dee, 1996.
Jiwani, Yasmin, Candis Steenbergen, and Claudia Mitchell, eds. *Girlhood: Redefining the Limits.* Montreal: Black Rose Books, 2006.
Jonas, Manfred. *Isolationism in America, 1935–1941.* Ithaca, N.Y.: Cornell University Press, 1966.
Jurika, Stephen, Jr., ed. *From Pearl Harbor to Vietnam: The Memoirs of Admiral Arthur W. Radford.* Stanford, Calif.: Hoover Institution Press, Stanford University, 1980.
Kee, Robert. *1945: The World We Fought For.* Boston: Little, Brown, 1985.
Kennedy, David M. *Freedom from Fear: The American People in Depression and War, 1929-1945.* New York: Oxford University Press, 1999.
Kennett, Lee. *For the Duration: The United States Goes to War, Pearl Harbor–1942.* New York: Charles Scribner's Sons, 1985.
Kersten, Andrew E. *Labor's Home Front: The American Federation of Labor during World War II.* New York: New York University Press, 2006.
Kessler, Lauren. *Stubborn Twig: Three Generations in the Life of a Japanese American Family.* New York: Random House, 1993.
Ketchum, Richard M. *The Borrowed Years, 1938–1941: America on the Way to War.* New York: Random House, 1993.
Kett, Joseph F. *Rites of Passage: Adolescence in America.* New York: Basic Books, 1977.
Kimble, Lionel, Jr. "I Too Serve America: African-American Women War Workers in Chicago, 1940–1945." *Journal of the Illinois State Historical Society* 93, no. 4 (Winter 2000–2001).
Kimmel, Husband E. *Admiral Kimmel's Story.* Chicago: Henry Regnery, 1955.
Kirk, Robert William. *Earning Their Stripes: The Mobilization of American Children in*

the Second World War. American University Studies series 9, History, vol. 156. New York: Peter Lang, 1994.

Koehler, Pat. "Reminiscence: The Women Ship Builders of World War II." *Oregon Historical Quarterly* 91, no. 3 (Fall 1990).

Kutulas, Judy. *The American Civil Liberties Union and the Making of Modern Liberalism, 1930–1960.* Chapel Hill: University of North Carolina Press, 2006.

LaForte, Robert E., and Ronald E. Marcello, eds. *Remembering Pearl Harbor: Eyewitness Accounts by U.S. Military Men and Women.* Wilmington, Del.: Scholarly Resources, 1991.

Lankton, Larry. "Autos to Armaments: Detroit Becomes the Arsenal of Democracy." *Michigan History Magazine* (November/December 1991).

Larrabee, Eric. *Commander in Chief: Franklin Delano Roosevelt, His Lieutenants, and Their War.* New York: Simon and Schuster, 1987.

Larson, George A. "Nebraska's World War II Bomber Plant: The Glenn L. Martin—Nebraska Company." *Nebraska History* 74 (Spring 1993).

Larson, T. A. *Wyoming's War Years, 1941–1945.* Laramie: University of Wyoming Press, 1954.

Lerner, Max. *Public Journal: Marginal Notes on Wartime America.* New York: Viking, 1945.

Levin, Diane E., and Nancy Carlsson-Paige. *The War Play Dilemma: What Every Parent and Teacher Needs to Know.* New York: Teachers College/Columbia University, 2006.

Lichtenstein, Nelson. *Labor's War at Home: The CIO in World War II.* Cambridge, Mass.: Cambridge University Press, 1982.

Lindenmeyer, Kriste. *The Greatest Generation Grows Up: American Childhood in the 1930s.* Chicago: Ivan R. Dee, 2005.

Litoff, Judy Barrett, and David C. Smith, eds. *American Women in a World at War: Contemporary Accounts from World War II.* Wilmington, Del.: Scholarly Resources, 1997.

Loew, Patty. "The Back of the Homefront: Black and American Indian Women in Wisconsin during World War II." *Wisconsin Magazine of History* 82, no. 2 (Winter 1998–1999).

Longmate, Norman. *How We Lived Then: A History of Everyday Life during the Second World War.* London: Pimlico, 2002.

Loo, Tai Sing. "How Happen I Were at Pearl Harbor on the Morning of Sunday, 7th of Dec. 1941." *United States Naval Institute Proceedings* (December 1962).

Lord, Walter. *Day of Infamy.* New York: Holt, Rinehart, and Winston, 1957.

Lukas, Richard C. *Did the Children Cry? Hitler's War against Jewish and Polish Children, 1939–1945.* New York: Hippocrene Books, 1994.

Macias, Richard. "'We All Had a Cause': Kansas City's Bomber Plant, 1941–1945." *Kansas History: A Journal of the Central Plains* 28, no. 4 (Winter 2005–2006).

Macleod, David I. *The Age of the Child: Children in America, 1890–1920.* New York: Twayne, 1998.

Makanaonalani, Dorinda. *Pearl Harbor Child: A Child's View of Pearl Harbor from Attack to Peace.* Kansas City, Mo.: Woodson House, 1993.

Marshall, Katherine Tupper. *Together: Annals of an Army Wife.* New York: Tupper and Love, 1946.
Marten, James. *The Children's Civil War.* Chapel Hill: University of North Carolina Press, 1998.
Mason, Theodore C. *Battleship Sailor.* Annapolis, Md.: Naval Institute Press, 1982.
Massey, Victoria. *One Child's War.* Whitstable, UK: Whitstable Litho, 1978.
Mazon, Mauricio. *The Zoot-Suit Riots: The Psychology of Symbolic Annihilation.* Austin: University of Texas Press, 1984.
McFarland, Keith D., and David L. Roll. *Louis Johnson and the Arming of America: The Roosevelt and Truman Years.* Bloomington: Indiana University Press, 2005.
McGoran, John W. "I Remember It Well." *Proceedings of the United States Naval Institute* (December 1979).
McGovern, Charles F. *Sold American: Consumption and Citizenship, 1890–1945.* Chapel Hill: University of North Carolina Press, 2006.
McGovern, James R. *And a Time for Hope: Americans in the Great Depression.* Westport, Conn.: Praeger, 2000.
McHaney, Sharon E. "Michigan Remembers 'The Longest Day.'" *Michigan History Magazine* (May/June 1994).
McRobbie, Angela, ed. *Zoot Suits and Second-Hand Dresses: An Anthology of Fashion and Music.* London: Macmillan Education, 1989.
McWilliams, Carey. *Ill Fares the Land: Migrants and Migratory Labor in the United States.* Boston: Little, Brown, 1942.
Mead, Harry. *Twenty Was Easy: Memoirs of a Pearl Harbor Survivor.* Charleston, S.C.: BookSurge, 2005.
"Memories from the Homefront: A Date which Will Live in Infamy." *Michigan History Magazine* (November/December 1991).
Merriam, Paul G., Thomas J. Molloy, and Theodore W. Sylvester Jr. *Home Front on Penobscot Bay: Rockland during the War Years, 1940–1945.* Rockland, Maine: Rockland Cooperative History Project, 1991.
Merrill, Francis E. *Social Problems on the Home Front: A Study of Wartime Influences.* New York: Harper and Brothers, 1948.
Mettler, Suzanne. *Soldiers to Citizens: The G.I. Bill and the Making of the Greatest Generation.* New York: Oxford University Press, 2005.
"Michigan Goes to War." *Michigan History Magazine* (March/April 1993).
Mickenberg, Julia L. *Learning from the Left: Children's Literature, the Cold War, and Radical Politics in the United States.* New York: Oxford University Press, 2006.
Milkman, Ruth. *Gender at Work: The Dynamics of Job Segregation by Sex during World War II.* Chicago: University of Illinois Press, 1987.
Miller, Marc Scott. *The Irony of Victory: World War II and Lowell, Massachusetts.* Urbana: University of Illinois Press, 1988.
Minns, Rayness. *Bombers and Mash: The Domestic Front, 1939–1945.* London: Virago Limited, 1980.
Mitchell, Claudia, and Jacqueline Reid-Walsh. *Researching Children's Popular Culture: The Cultural Spaces of Childhood.* London: Routledge, 2002.
Mitchell, Claudia, and Jacqueline Reid-Walsh, eds. *Seven Going on Seventeen: Tween*

Studies in the Culture of Girlhood. New York: Peter Lang, 2005.

Mullener, Elizabeth. *War Stories: Remembering World War II.* New York: Berkley Books, 2002.

Myhre, Ethelyn. *Hawaiian Yesterdays.* New York: Alfred A. Knopf, 1942.

Nash, Ilana. *American Sweethearts: Teenage Girls in Twentieth-Century Popular Culture.* Bloomington: Indiana University Press, 2006.

Nicholson, H. V. *Prisoners of War: True Stories of Evacuees/Their Lost Childhood.* London: Gordon Publishing, 2000.

Noake, Jeremy. *The Civilian in War: The Home Front in Europe, Japan, and the USA in World War II.* Exeter, UK: University of Exeter Press, 1992.

Noble, Annette Chambers. "Utah's Rosies: Women in the Utah War Industries during World War II." *Utah Historical Quarterly* 59 (Spring 1991).

O'Brien, Kenneth Paul, and Lynn Hudson Parsons. *The Home-Front War: World War II and American Society.* Contributions in American History, number 161. Westport, Conn.: Greenwood Press, 1995.

O'Brien, Patrick G. "Kansas at War: The Home Front, 1941–1945." *Kansas History* 17, no. 1 (Spring 1994).

Okumiya, Masatake, and Jiro Horikoshi with Martin Caidin. *Zero!* New York: E. P. Dutton, 1956.

O'Neill, William L. *A Democracy at War: America's Fight at Home and Abroad in World War II.* Cambridge, Mass.: Harvard University Press, 1993.

Osgood, Charles. *Defending Baltimore against Enemy Attack: A Boyhood Year during World War II.* New York: Hyperion, 2004.

Oshinsky, David M. *Polio: An American Story. The Crusade that Mobilized the Nation against the Twentieth Century's Most Feared Disease.* New York: Oxford University Press, 2005.

Overy, Richard. *Why the Allies Won.* New York: W. W. Norton, 1995.

Pagan, Eduardo Obregon. *Murder at the Sleepy Lagoon: Zoot Suits, Race, and Riot in Wartime L.A.* Chapel Hill: University of North Carolina Press, 2003.

Parker, Matthew. *Monte Cassino: The Hardest-Fought Battle of World War II.* New York: Doubleday, 2004.

Parrish, Thomas. *Roosevelt and Marshall: Partners in Politics and War.* New York: William Morrow, 1989.

Patri, Angelo. *Your Children in Wartime.* Garden City, N.Y.: Doubleday, Doran, 1943.

Pearson, Rudy. "'A Menace to the Neighborhood': Housing and African Americans in Portland, 1941–1945." *Oregon Historical Quarterly* 102, no. 2 (Summer 2001).

Peterson, Louis, as told to Clarke Van Vleet. "I Was There . . . and Remember Pearl Harbor, December 7, 1941." *Naval Aviation News* (December 1981).

Phylon: The Atlanta University Review of Race and Culture 4, no. 2 (1943).

Polenberg, Richard. *America at War: The Home Front, 1941–1945.* Englewood Cliffs, N.J.: Prentice Hall, 1968.

———. "The Good War? A Reappraisal of How World War II Affected American Society." *Virginia Magazine of History and Biography* 100 (July 1992).

Prange, Gordon W., with Donald M. Goldstein and Katherine V. Dillon. *At Dawn We Slept: The Untold Story of Pearl Harbor.* New York: Penguin, 1981.

———. *December 7, 1941: The Day the Japanese Attacked Pearl Harbor.* New York: McGraw-Hill Book Company, 1988.

———. *God's Samurai: Lead Pilot at Pearl Harbor.* Washington, D.C.: Brassey's, 1990.

Pyle, Ernie. *Here Is Your War.* New York: Henry Holt, 1943.

Raymer, Edward C. *Descent into Darkness: Pearl Harbor, 1941: A Navy Diver's Memoir.* Novato, Calif.: Presidio Press, 1996.

Rempel, Gerhard. *Hitler's Children: The Hitler Youth and the SS.* Chapel Hill: University of North Carolina Press, 1989.

Reynolds, David. *From Munich to Pearl Harbor: Roosevelt's America and the Origins of the Second World War.* Chicago: Ivan R. Dee, 2001.

Richardson, K. D. *Reflections of Pearl Harbor: An Oral History of December 7, 1941.* Westport, Conn.: Praeger, 2005.

Riley, Karen L. *Schools behind Barbed Wire: The Untold Story of Wartime Internment and the Children of Arrested Enemy Aliens.* New York: Rowman and Littlefield, 2002.

Riney-Kehrberg, Pamela. *Childhood on the Farm: Work, Play, and Coming of Age in the Midwest.* Lawrence: University Press of Kansas, 2005.

———. "Helping Ma and Helping Pa: Iowa's Turn-of-the-Century Farm Children," *Annals of Iowa* 59 (Spring 2000).

Robins, Phil, ed. *Under Fire: Children of the Second World War Tell Their Stories.* In association with the Imperial War Museum. London: Scholastic, 2004.

Rupp, Leila J. *Mobilizing Women for War: German and American Propaganda, 1939–1945.* Princeton, N.J.: Princeton University Press, 1978.

Russell, Beverly. "World War II Boomtown: Hastings and the Naval Ammunition Depot." *Nebraska History* 76, nos. 2–3 (Summer/Fall 1995).

Russell, Henry Dozier. *Pearl Harbor Story.* Macon, Ga.: Mercer University Press, 2001.

Sakamaki, Kazuo. *I Attacked Pearl Harbor.* Translated by Toru Matsumoto. New York: Association Press, 1949.

Satterfield, Archie. *The Day the War Began.* Westport, Conn.: Praeger, 1992.

———. *The Home Front: An Oral History of the War Years in America, 1941–1945.* New York: Playboy Press, 1981.

Savage, Jon. *Teenage: The Creation of Youth Culture.* New York: Viking, 2007.

Schoen, Johanna. *Choice and Coercion: Birth Control, Sterilization, and Abortion in Public Health and Welfare.* Chapel Hill: University of North Carolina Press, 2005.

Segrave, Kerry. *Jukeboxes: An American Social History.* Jefferson, N.C.: McFarland, 2002.

Seidman, Joel. *American Labor from Defense to Reconversion.* Chicago: University of Chicago Press, 1953.

Shell, Marc. *Polio and Its Aftermath: The Paralysis of Culture.* Cambridge, Mass.: Harvard University Press, 2005.

Sitton, Tom. *Los Angeles Transformed: Fletcher Bowron's Urban Reform Revival, 1938–1953.* Albuquerque: University of New Mexico Press, 2005.

Smith, Bruce C. *The War Comes to Plum Street.* Bloomington: Indiana University Press, 2005.

Smith, C. Calvin. *War and Wartime Changes: The Transformation of Arkansas, 1940–1945.* Fayetteville: University of Arkansas Press, 1986.

Smith, Carl. *Pearl Harbor: The Day of Infamy.* Oxford, UK: Osprey Publishing, 2001.

Stafford, David. *Roosevelt and Churchill: Men of Secrets.* New York: Overlook Press, 2000.

Stalcup, Ann. *On the Home Front: Growing Up in Wartime England.* North Haven, Conn.: Linnet Books, 1998.

Starett, Ann. "Rationing Is Women's Job." *Independent Woman* (May 1942).

Steele, Evelyn. *Wartime Opportunities for Women.* New York: E. P. Dutton, 1943.

Stoler, Mark A., and Melanie S. Gustafson, eds. *Major Problems in the History of World War II.* Boston: Houghton Mifflin, 2003.

Stromquist, Shelton. *Solidarity and Survival: An Oral History of Iowa Labor in the Twentieth Century.* Iowa City: University of Iowa Press, 1993.

Sullivan, George. *The Day Pearl Harbor Was Bombed: A Photo History of World War II.* New York: Scholastic, 1991.

Terkel, Studs. *"The Good War": An Oral History of World War II.* New York: New Press, 1984.

Thomas, Mary Martha. *Riveting and Rationing in Dixie: Alabama Women and the Second World War.* Tuscaloosa: University of Alabama Press, 1987.

Toland, John. *Infamy: Pearl Harbor and Its Aftermath.* Garden City, N.Y.: Doubleday, 1982.

Tucker, Barbara M. "Agricultural Workers in World War II: The Reserve Army of Children, Black Americans, and Jamaicans." *Agricultural History* 68 (Winter 1994).

Tuttle, William M., Jr. *"Daddy's Gone to War": The Second World War in the Lives of America's Children.* New York: Oxford University Press, 1993.

Valdez, Luis. *Zoot Suit and Other Plays.* Houston: Arte Publico Press, 1992.

Walton, Francis. *Miracle of World War II: How American Industry Made Victory Possible.* New York: Macmillan, 1956.

"Wartime Internment." *Journal of American History* 77, no. 2 (September 1990).

Watt, Donald Cameron. *How War Came: The Immediate Origins of the Second World War, 1938–1939.* London: William Heinemann, 1989.

Weatherford, Doris. *American Women and World War II.* New York: Facts on File, 1990.

Webb, Daryl. "Scooters, Skates, and Dolls: Toys against Delinquency in Milwaukee." *Wisconsin Magazine of History* (Summer 2004).

Werner, Emmy E. *Through the Eyes of Innocents: Children Witness World War II.* Boulder, Colo.: Westview Press, 2000.

West, Elliot, and Paula Petrik, eds. *Small Worlds: Children and Adolescents in America, 1850–1950.* Lawrence: University of Kansas Press, 1992.

Westerlund, John S. "Bombs from Bellemont: Navajo Ordnance Depot in World War II." *Journal of Arizona History* 42, no. 3 (Autumn 2001).

Williams, Carol Traynor. *The Dream beside Me: The Movies and the Children of the Forties.* London: Associated University Presses, 1980.
Winkler, Allan. *Home Front U.S.A.* Arlington Heights, Ill.: H. Davidson, 1986.
Winnicott, D. W. *Deprivation and Delinquency.* London: Tavistock, 1984.
Wise, Nancy Baker. *A Mouthful of Rivets: Women at Work in World War II.* San Francisco: Jossey-Bass, 1994.
Wohlstetter, Roberta. *Pearl Harbor: Warning and Decision.* Stanford, Calif.: Stanford University Press, 1962.
Wolf, Anna W. M. *Our Children Face War.* Boston: Houghton Mifflin, 1942.
Wood, Sharon E. *The Freedom of the Streets: Work, Citizenship, and Sexuality in a Gilded Age City.* Chapel Hill: University of North Carolina Press, 2005.
Zelizer, Viviana A. *Pricing the Priceless Child: The Changing Social Value of Children.* New York: Basic Books, 1985.
Ziemer, Gregor. *Education for Death: The Making of the Nazi.* London: Oxford University Press, 1941.
Zwicky, John. "A State at War: The Home Front in Illinois during the Second World War." PhD diss., Loyola University of Chicago, 1989.

Index